Motherhood
after
Miscarriage

Dr. Kathleen Diamond

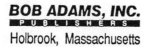

BOB ADAMS, INC.
PUBLISHERS
Holbrook, Massachusetts

Published by Bob Adams, Inc.
260 Center Street, Holbrook, MA 02343

ISBN: 1-55850-043-X

Printed in the United States of America

B C D E F G H I J

This publication is designed to provide accurate and authoritative information with regard to the subject matter covered. It is sold with the understanding that the publisher is not engaged in rendering legal, accounting, or other professional advice. If legal advice or other expert assistance is required, the services of a qualified professional person should be sought.
— From a *Declaration of Principles* jointly adopted by a Committee of the American Bar Association and a Committee of Publishers and Associations.

Dedicated with love
to Pete,
Lena and Karl,
and
to every woman
who ever wanted to be a mother.

Acknowledgments

MY EARLY ENDEAVORS IN LIFE were eased along by the fact that my older sister went through them first and let me know what to expect. Eventually, there came some experiences that I had to stumble through unprepared. The intent of this book is to share my stumblings through miscarriage and ease the way for other women. At the same time, this book has only been possible because of the many women who have shared their experiences with me. I thank those who told me their stories of miscarriage, of struggling to have their children; they are the greatest contributors to this book.

I also wrote this book to finish working out my own sorrows. I can hardly feel my own miscarriage pain anymore, but by sharing I have become sensitive to the losses of others—and I now feel each woman's sorrow as if it were my own.

Thanks to Dr. Deborah Joy for that first phone call. I realized that I had something important to share, and that it was time to get to work. Thanks to Andrea Winden and Jennifer Walton for reading the early chapters and giving me confidence to continue. Thanks to Dr. Kelly Star for reading almost every page of every draft and offering insightful and enthusiastic praise. Thanks to my brother Todd Walton for always encouraging me, always expressing optimism, and (not least) for introducing me to my agent Patti Breitman. Thanks to Patti for believing in the work and for staying with it, and for finding the right publisher in Bob Adams. Thanks to my editors Katherine Layzer and Brandon Toropov, and to the staff at Bob Adams for putting it all together.

Gratitude is also due to the obstetricians who answered my

questionnaire on miscarriage. My appreciation goes to Dr. Robert Nachtigall for reading the medical chapters and helping me to make them clear and accurate. Thanks to Dr. Robert Glass for his very useful text on reproductive hormones and for discussing my many questions. Thanks to Dr. Gilbert Webb for reading the book—though our approaches and opinions differ.

I must also thank my parents, Dr. Charles Walton and Avis Walton, for everything. Thanks to my sister Wendy Dickerman, and my brothers Todd and Steve Walton, for sending hopeful thoughts my way through every pregnancy and for being excited about the book. And thanks to my patient, constant husband and our wonderful children for giving me joy and letting me snatch moments and hours away from them to write this book.

Table of Contents

Part I
Experiencing and coping with a miscarriage

Part II
Biology of early pregnancy

Part III
Why did this happen? Explaining and preventing miscarriage

Part IV
Appendices

Introduction

WELCOME TO A LONELY CLUB. The sorrow of miscarriage is private. It is usually accompanied by a feeling of ignorance, and sometimes shame. Though countless women have miscarriages, there is no strength in their numbers. Many feel unworthy, alone, unreliable. Often women believe their bodies have failed them, and they in turn have failed their families. In addition, other people may not acknowledge the grief these women suffer for their lost child.

There is little sympathy in our society for early pregnancy loss. Information is difficult to obtain and understand. Most obstetricians will say, "It's for the best. At least you know you can get pregnant." It is true that the vast majority of women who have one miscarriage go on to have a baby. It is true that most miscarriages can never be explained. But women, and their mates, need to know that their grief is legitimate. An expected baby can have a very real existence in its mother's mind. Women need to know there are others who sympathize with the physical and emotional pain of their experience. Couples want some explanation for their loss. In our technological society, where we read of new medical miracles every day, it is hard to believe that so little can be offered to the woman who encounters this obstacle to motherhood.

Those of us who have been through miscarriage can offer our emotional support to others. When I had my first miscarriage, I did not know anyone else who had miscarried. As a biologist, I thought I understood and accepted it, but emotionally I found myself at sea. If I could have shared my experience with another woman who had been through it, it would have helped me. Talking over one's grief and feelings of guilt and failure with sympathetic others seems to be the best approach to getting over a miscarriage.

After several miscarriages, I became terribly uncertain. I wanted to know why women miscarry, and why some women miscarry several times. I found that medical knowledge and interest is spotty. Individual doctors consider and may treat one or a few possible causes. Different doctors have different "favorites." I started to work on a summary of the known causes and current treatments to prevent miscarriage from recurring. As I told people of my plans to write about this, more and more women sought me out. I found that the emotional side of their experience was bound up with their desire for an explanation of what happened. So I decided to address both the emotional and biological issues.

This book is organized into three parts. Part I, "Experiencing and coping with a miscarriage," offers moving stories and practical advice, addressing the physical experience itself and the emotional aftermath. It includes a personal account of my first miscarriage. Though my account is individual, it contains some common themes. It also provides a window for people who have not had a miscarriage to see what many of us have experienced. Next I relate the range of physical and medical experiences that can occur during a miscarriage. I describe the spectrum of feelings women have afterwards, and their efforts to get through this rough emotional ride.

I also address the emotional concerns of the small number of women who have a series of miscarriages, or miscarry after a hard-to-achieve pregnancy. Part I includes a personal account of my own series of miscarriages and the experiences of other women who have coped with this particular fertility problem. Even women who miscarry many times have a very good chance of having children.

Part II, "Biology of early pregnancy," provides some general background on events in a woman's body as she prepares for and begins a pregnancy. I explain the important role that hormones play in getting and staying pregnant. I explain that pregnancy loss is more common than the often-heard "one out of five," and, in fact, may occur in one of every two conceptions. I try to put miscarriage into perspective as a normal part of our human inheritance.

Part III, "Why did this happen? Explaining and preventing miscarriage," is compiled from medical journals, current texts, and discussions with obstetricians. I describe the causes of miscarriage, from the common to the rare, from well established to just probable. This includes genetic mistakes, which explain most one-time miscarriages and a small percentage of recurrent miscarriages. Current medical approaches to preventing recurrent miscarriages are described. I discuss hormone deficiencies and excesses, physical problems of the uterus, infections, immune problems, and others.

In Part III, I also discuss the increasing miscarriage risks of women over thirty-five, and the need for a small percentage of women to consider alternatives to biological motherhood. Part III attempts to give some satisfactory answers to questions raised by women after one miscarriage. It is also intended to encourage women who have multiple miscarriages to seek answers and real help from their doctors. In a separate appendix I explain more about hormone treatments for infertility.

My goal in writing this book is to give comfort and information to any woman who has had a miscarriage. While offering strong emotional support and guidance, the book presents nontechnical explanations of the biology of pregnancy and the causes of miscarriage. Drawing on my personal experience with miscarriage and my career in biology, I have tried to create a book that is both sensitive and sensible. This book is intended to let a woman know she is not alone, not unworthy, not a failure. Rather, she is a normal, typical human with a very good chance of having a successful pregnancy. She is entitled to our sympathy, and to our respect for her deep-rooted wish to be a mother, in spite of setbacks along the way. It is her right to have realistic expectations when she is pregnant again. The support of others who have suffered similarly, and the knowledge of what is going on in her body, can restore her confidence and help her get back on the road to motherhood.

Part I

Experiencing and Coping with a Miscarriage

Chapter 1

Miscarriage Before Childbirth: A Personal Account

EVERY WOMAN SHOULD HAVE THE CHANCE to tell the story of her miscarriage to a sympathetic audience. Retelling it brings back all the emotions, and so it is painful, but every retelling helps the healing, whether the miscarriage happened a week or many years ago. Every woman's miscarriage story contains some experiences and emotions that are almost universal and some that are unique. Some parts of the story are hard to talk about; some parts cannot be told.

In this chapter I will describe the events and emotions of my first miscarriage. Although the details of my account are unique, every woman may recognize some aspect of my experience as similar to her own. I hope my account will set an example of sharing for women who are holding it in and help them find someone to tell their story to—even the pages of a private journal. For men and women who have family or friends who have miscarried, the details of my experience may help them understand it all a little better.

The physical and emotional ordeal of miscarriage is particularly upsetting if it occurs before a woman has had a child, as was my case. Since I had not had a full-term pregnancy, I could not expect or deal with the strong uterine contractions, similar to the labor of childbirth, that can occur during a miscarriage. The experience was frightening. It was quite painful and surprisingly bloody. This is often the rule when a pregnancy has lasted at least 10 weeks (8 weeks after conception*).

When having a baby, a woman tells herself the pain is for a good cause and will end with the delivery of her baby. During a miscarriage the pain is for no good reason, signifies a terrible loss, and will usually end when a D and C is performed (D and C is dilation of the cervix and curettage, scraping the walls of the uterus). I had a D and C at the emergency room, but it may also be done in a doctor's office.

I was 14 weeks pregnant but barely showing, a typical first-pregnancy condition. I had told very few people, and it was my private joke: how long before someone would figure it out, or be nervy enough to ask about that little tummy. I had not yet told my department chairman at the university, but I was about to have a meeting with a colleague to schedule a jointly taught class.

Without telling her the reason, since I did not know her well, I wanted to schedule my lectures so as not to be teaching during the weeks before and after my due date.

Just before the appointment I went to the bathroom and saw a ghostly pale-pink spot on the toilet tissue. I blinked my eyes and caught my breath. Never in the middle of any monthly cycle, nor during 14 weeks of pregnancy, had I ever spotted. I felt certain this could only mean one thing: I was going to lose the baby. Stifling hysteria, I returned numbly to my office and, feeling quite foolish, went through with the scheduling to avoid what now seemed an imaginary due date. When the professor asked the reason for the special scheduling, I mumbled something about a medical procedure.

After the meeting I called my best friend. She was worried

* Many doctors use "menstruation age" for length of pregnancy. The pregnancy is measured in the number of weeks from the start of the last menstrual period. By this measure pregnancy lasts 40 weeks, although human development time is actually 38 weeks. This is a bit ridiculous, because it means a woman is two weeks pregnant on the day of conception! However, it is the traditional means of dating pregnancies, since it used to be impossible to pinpoint the day of conception. In this book I will use this means of dating a pregnancy, and I will usually mention the actual (probable) time since conception, for clarity.

but tried to be upbeat. I thought she sounded very sorry. I called my obstetrics office and was told to relax and wait; many women spot during pregnancy. Later I called the emergency room and was told not to come in until I was bleeding enough to go through a heavy menstrual pad within half an hour. I went home feeling doomed, though I had stopped spotting and had not had any cramps. My husband was impatient with my worries. "Just relax. You're building this up in your mind. It's nothing." If I could somehow stop worrying I would not have a miscarriage. But if I kept worrying and had a miscarriage, would it be my fault?

My husband and I had rented a house in anticipation of the baby, and we were going to move in in two days. The light spotting began again in the evening, while I lay dumbly looking up at the ceiling. Spotting continued in the morning, and I started having mild cramps when my husband left for work. I had to go to the new house to wait for the gas man to come. I called a friend and told her I thought I was having a miscarriage. She said, "I'll meet you at the house. I'll be there soon." The cramps became stronger while I drove. I gasped, gripped the wheel, and went on ahead, trying to will them away. By the time I got to the house I could not have driven any further. We did not have a phone yet. My friend was late. The pain was unexpected and seemed unbearable. I did not know what to do about it. I moaned and hollered, literally rolling all over the floor through the empty rooms of the house. I felt like an animal, with all human qualities lost. The gas man rang the bell, and I opened the door from the floor. "Er, are you all right?" "I'm having a miscarriage." "Perhaps I'll come back when you're feeling better."

It seemed like years before my friend arrived. She took me right to the emergency room. Though I was not bleeding very heavily, the contractions were strong. While I waited to be examined, I went to the rest room, and suddenly delivered a pale little birdlike fetus, about three inches long. There was no blood with it. It was pure white. I shakily retrieved it from the toilet and wrapped its lifeless form in tissue to show to the doctor. I wasn't sure how closely I should study this little white thing. I felt ashamed trying to see if it had been a boy or girl. I thought it was a girl, but it seemed more like a bird than a person. I sat in the waiting room a few more minutes with the little paper towel package, then returned to the rest room and threw up.

The nurse and gynecologist seemed kind and gentle during the D and C. They gave me intravenous Valium, one of the side effects of which is amnesia. So when my husband came from work to see how I was doing, I tearfully told him I was still waiting for the procedure. My physical recovery from the miscarriage was fast. I took things a little easier for a few days. I knew I was doing too much whenever the bleeding became heavy.

I did not change any of our plans for the weekend. I later learned that other women often feel the need to carry on without missing a beat after a miscarriage. The day after my miscarriage I helped move lightweight things while my husband and a friend did all the major work. The couple who were helping us move were my husband's friends, and I did not particularly care for them. It gave me a grim and perverse satisfaction, a combination of self-punishment and self-righteousness, to keep the news of the miscarriage from these people during the move and lunch. They had not known I was pregnant. I felt they thought of me as very lazy to be helping hardly at all with the move. I thought of them as the densest people I had ever known. Actually they are quite sweet and caring people, but they were tainted with the anger I directed at the world and myself at the time. Though they were innocent bystanders, to this day I cannot stand them.

The same day we moved, we went to a big evening wedding an hour's drive away. I felt I had to go about business as usual, to pretend nothing had happened. The whole experience had an aura of unreality. It seemed stupid to tell people who had not known that I was pregnant that I had miscarried, so I suffered alone. I soon realized what a mistake this was. I became very angry at everyone around me, as if they were forcing me to go on with ordinary activities. But of course none of them, except my husband, even knew.

The emotional pain of my miscarriage was tied up with my struggle to have children. While many couples were struggling with fertility problems, others, like us, battled over the decision to have children at all. I was ready to have children before I even met my husband. Like many women of my generation, I had been married in my early twenties, then divorced. After being on my own for several years, I knew I could give up my independence for the right man. When I met my future husband I was already sure I wanted to have children, but I knew I would have to be patient for a few years. When we were first dating, I told him, "What you see is not all you get. I come with two kids. You can't see them, but they are part of me." I took on the care of his dog, and expected that his continued interest in me meant he accepted our unborn children.

After we had been together a few years, I began to press him for a child. I wanted children much more now that I knew and loved their father. One spring I had a complete obstetrics work-up and had my IUD removed. I told my husband that the doctor had said I needed to let my uterus recover from thirteen years of IUD use, just for general health reasons. In fact my obstetrician has suggested that I have the IUD taken out a few months before trying to get pregnant.

That summer my husband did not enjoy sex. He was very careful to use a condom all the time and did not trust any spontaneity on my part. We were on a sailing cruise, and I had hoped the romance of the sea would win him over, and that we might conceive our child on the boat. When we returned home at the end of the summer, I tried again to convince him to have a child, but he was adamantly opposed. So I offered to get a new IUD if he would consider our getting pregnant in the spring. He agreed, and a few months later he also agreed to come with me to a psychologist, to see if we could talk over our differences on the parenting matter. What a nightmare that turned out to be. Our health plan did not give us much choice in therapists, and we did not really know what we were looking for. I thought some conversations in neutral territory might open some doors between us. The psychologist did not seem to know what to do with us. We said things to each other that should only be told in private. We both came away feeling poisoned and ill. There was no

growth or insight, only terrible hurt. Finally we stopped going;
we had suffered enough. I saw no hope for a baby.

It was spring again and my husband refused to have a child.
I looked at my choices. I could strike out on my own, find a
sperm donor and be a single mother. I could wait and hope and
get older and angrier. Or I could secretly get my IUD taken out,
and this was what I chose. I got pregnant the next month. When
I was sure, I sat my husband down and told him. I apologized
and told him I loved him, but I was beyond desperation. He said,
"Well, we'd better look for a house."

It was difficult dealing with the difference between our feelings about my pregnancy, then miscarriage. I felt hurt by his in-
difference, actually relief, at the miscarriage. But I also felt guilty
for having tricked him into the pregnancy. To me, miscarriage
was my punishment for tricking him into the pregnancy, and it
was a cosmic correction of a wrong situation: a baby unwanted
by its father. He was not happy about the pregnancy, and he was
impatient with my worries when I started spotting. But when he
came to see me in the emergency room, and later to take me
home, he was sweet and sympathetic. After that it seemed he
had no further concerns.

In fact, his reaction to the miscarriage was neutral, for the
most part. He was relieved of the burden of expecting a child he
did not want, but he knew I had wanted it badly. He knew better
than to rub it in. But about six weeks later we went out of town
to visit an old close friend of his. As the two couples sat around
the table, the friend asked how we had been. My husband cheer-
fully answered, "Great!" I embarrassed all of us by objecting,
blurting out that I had had a miscarriage and that my husband
was happy about it. The visit became strained after that. This
couple did not want to witness our conflicts and sorrows.

Some books about pregnancy and childbirth make the obser-
vation that men often do not become involved with a pregnancy
until it is well advanced; some men not until childbirth classes or
the delivery itself. It should not be surprising that after a miscarriage, many women will be mourning losses that are not even
perceived as such by their mates. Certainly my response to mis-

carriage cannot be separated from my struggle to have children with my husband. Some women will not identify with this. But most women who miscarry find that they do not get enough support even from very caring husbands, simply because only another woman who has miscarried can really understand. There is a spectrum of men's and women's responses, and each couple has its own unique combination along the spectrum, as we will see in chapter 3.

For three months after the miscarriage I mourned a lost child. I had to frame some tapestries I had woven for an art fair, and I would go on long crying binges while working on them and listening to music. My favorite for sobbing was Jim Kweskin singing "Amelia Earhart's Last Flight." In those days the hardest thing was seeing pregnant women, especially very young ones, who looked to me as if they had no appreciation of their miraculous state. Though not religious, I imagined my little dead child going to keep my grandmother company and bring her news of the world. My due date had been my dead grandfather's birthday, and I had told my grandmother I was pregnant just a week before she died.

I was sorry that I did not have more company in my loss, and wished I had told more people that I had been pregnant. My parents, brothers, and sister had known I was pregnant and had been very excited. Everyone in the family knew I had wanted children for years, and the baby was eagerly awaited. They were all saddened by my loss, and each called and sent me lovely letters. Since they all lived several hundred miles away, however, there was no real physical presence to support me. My family has always considered me pretty tough and independent, so they probably perceived that my needs were slight anyway. No one I knew had ever had a miscarriage, and I was too timid to seek out another woman who had, though I could have done so through friends.

Over the next month my family and the few friends who did know I had miscarried asked me again and again if my doctor had told us why it happened, or if he was trying to determine why. I found myself assuring all of them that there was no need to worry. The doctor was not concerned about seeking a cause, and we assumed it was just bad luck, a fairly common and even minor mishap. I had gotten pregnant once; I would get pregnant again.

Without any doctor telling me, I guessed that the miscarriage occurred because of simple bad luck. A genetically deficient embryo had been formed, probably because of my thirty-five-year-old egg. The abnormal embryo had died early in development. However, I suspected there was some chance that my uterus might not have provided a good environment for the embryo, since I had used IUDs continuously for 13 years and had gotten pregnant only one month after the last was removed. In either case, we could not get any more information, and there was no reason to think I would have another miscarriage.

I did not feel a need for therapy. I was going through a healthy mourning for my loss. My main concern was getting pregnant again. I waited impatiently to start my period, so I would know I was fertile again. After more than 10 weeks of pregnancy, about 6 weeks usually pass before the first menstrual period—thus 4 weeks until the release of an egg. During this wait I did not lose the extra weight I had gained during that 14-week pregnancy. It was too depressing to lose that little tummy when I wanted to be pregnant so badly. The weight stayed on through my next pregnancy.

My husband did not want to try for another pregnancy. But after a few months, by some miracle he gave in. Maybe he got tired of listening to my weeping pleas. Or maybe he wanted to be closer to me after we came home from a depressing Christmas party. Now, at least, I could stop my desperate plotting of new ways to get around his refusals. I got pregnant three months after the miscarriage, and was torn between wanting everyone to know and not wanting to get excited too early. I wanted to have more support if I lost another baby. So I told a few more people than before, and also told them I had miscarried. I needed to have them know what had happened to me, even after the fact. I wanted as many people sending hopeful wishes in my direction as possible.

Overall, I assumed that one miscarriage is quite common but the chances of a second pretty slim. I rationalized that it had not been right to get pregnant without my husband's consent and that it was better that we not start off our family in this way. This second pregnancy was better because we both agreed, though to different degrees. I did not curtail my activities in any way, except when I felt tired. I was working and exercising normally, guided only by my body's feelings, not any concerns about miscarrying. I still had my age to concern me, and I waited anxiously until after the results of amniocentesis came in at about 19 weeks; then I became hopeful. I had an easy pregnancy and gave birth to my lovely daughter, one week early, on Labor Day.

Chapter 2

The Physical Experience of Miscarriage

A MISCARRIAGE IS A PHYSICAL AND EMOTIONAL TRAUMA. Although it is usually not considered a serious medical situation, it can be painful, confusing, and frightening for the individual. There is so little discussion of miscarriage in our society that women do not know what to expect when they begin to miscarry. Many are not even sure they are having a miscarriage. To prepare for childbirth, couples often read a variety of how-to books and take childbirth classes. There are no classes to prepare for miscarriage. No one ever expects to miscarry. When a woman starts to miscarry, it is unscheduled, unprepared-for, and unpredictable. It is a shock to the body and the mind.

Although the physical and emotional aspects of miscarriage are often bound together, I will discuss the experiences women have with the medical event first and how women deal with the emotional aftermath second, in chapter 3. Women have a range of experiences during the physical process of miscarriage. As with any trauma, sharing experiences with others can be therapeutic. This chapter provides an opportunity for women who have miscarried to compare notes. In addition I will explain miscarriage from the medical point of view, to help women see why their obstetricians made certain decisions and how the course of their miscarriage compares to others'.

Whatever her long-term feelings about her lost baby or failed pregnancy, a woman has the additional memory of her own physical trauma. Many lingering emotions are associated with the medical event itself. Many women have frightening and confusing experiences in the emergency room. They often encounter medical people who are not aware that this is an ordeal.

> My husband was out of town. I tried to call him but I couldn't reach him. I wanted to talk to him so badly. I didn't even want to go to the hospital without talking to him. Then I started passing blood clots and knew that I had to go to the hospital. I had already had a D and C by the time my husband knew about it. I spent the night at the hospital. He was there in the morning. We were both Rh negative, and I refused the Rhogam injection, but one of the doctors said, "If your husband is not the father of the child this could be very dangerous." I was outraged. It took forever to get out of the hospital because I wouldn't take their injection. Then they billed me for it anyway.

After a woman miscarries, she is often caught between her shock and other people's lack of awareness. To the outside world nothing much has happened. She has not been sick or injured. She might not have looked pregnant up to her miscarriage, and she looks no different the next day. She is often able to go about business as usual. Yet privately she has suffered, and will continue to suffer.

There is great variation in the duration, degree of pain, and amount of bleeding that make up the physical process of miscarriage. While there is some correlation between length of the pregnancy and the amount of pain and bleeding, it is not absolute. Some women deliver a recognizable fetus. Many do not. Many women are seen by a doctor and have a D and C performed; others go through the whole miscarriage at home. Some variations in the medical experience are due to the time and nature of the individual miscarriage. Others are due to personal choices of women or their doctors.

Three out of four clinically reported miscarriages occur before 12 weeks (10 weeks after conception), and most of these are between 8 and 12 weeks. Most late miscarriages, those after 12 weeks, occur before 16 weeks. Miscarriage, is defined by different obstetricians as loss of pregnancy before 20 weeks, 24 weeks, or 28 weeks, or simply before the baby can survive on its own. Since pregnancy loss between 20 and 27 weeks is very rare, any of these definitions includes almost all miscarriages. Physicians use the term spontaneous abortion (SAB on one's chart), but I will use the term miscarriage exclusively.

For a woman to understand what is going on in her body during a miscarriage, she needs to know what is happening in the pregnancy at that time. The egg is released from the ovary about 14 days before the start of the next menstrual period. Conception can occur on the day of ovulation or the day after. The embryo arrives in the uterus 4 to 5 days later. It begins to implant in the wall of the uterus 6 to 7 days after leaving the ovary. The placenta begins to form from the embryo's own tissues and the lining of the uterus. Those of the embryo's cells that will develop into the placenta start releasing the pregnancy hormone HCG beginning about 9 days after conception. By 12 weeks, the placenta is fully developed into a complex organ deeply entrenched in the uterus. The developing baby is called an embryo for 8 weeks (6 weeks after conception), and a fetus starting about 9 weeks. Figures 1, 2, 3, and 4 show early human development at 2, 4, 6, and 8 weeks after conception.

The placenta is a unique organ found only in mammals. It is a joint effort, made of tissues from the mother and the developing baby. It is a major hormone-producing gland for about seven months, producing large quantities of estrogen, progesterone, and other hormones. The mother's and baby's blood vessels flow side by side in the placenta, and various substances are exchanged back and forth between the two bloodstreams. Through placental blood vessels the mother supplies the baby with digested food and oxygen, as well as immune protection against disease. The mother's blood takes away carbon dioxide (which we normally exhale through our lungs), and digestive wastes to be excreted. Unfortunately, the mother can also deliver disease-causing viruses, alcohol, nicotine, cocaine, and many other drugs and toxins to the baby through the placenta. These can interfere with normal development, and in some cases cause miscarriage.

A miscarriage at 4-7 weeks (2-5 weeks after conception) is similar to a menstrual period, though there is usually more

FIGURE 1. Human embryo at 2 weeks after fertilization (about 4 weeks of pregnancy). Tissue layers are just forming. There is no outside or inside yet. The future brain is beginning to form from ridges of tissue called neural folds. Tissue blocks in the center will form the vertebral column. During the next week the heart will form and start beating. Actual size is about one-eighth of an inch.

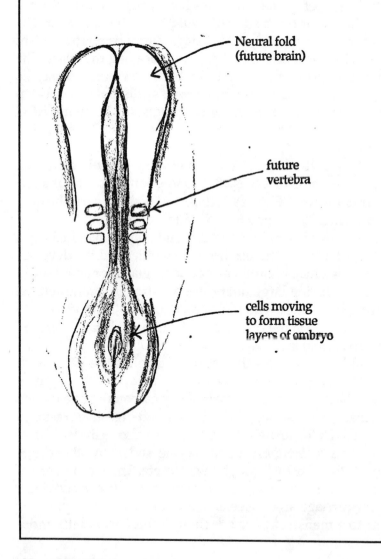

Neural fold
(future brain)

future
vertebra

cells moving
to form tissue
layers of embryo

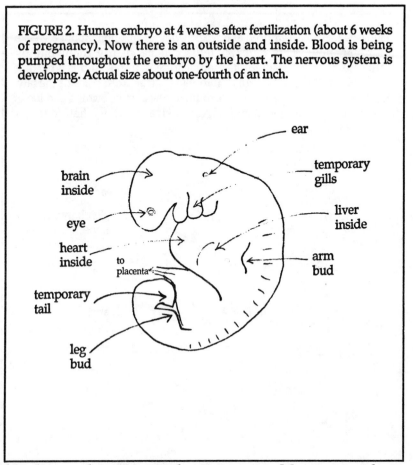

FIGURE 2. Human embryo at 4 weeks after fertilization (about 6 weeks of pregnancy). Now there is an outside and inside. Blood is being pumped throughout the embryo by the heart. The nervous system is developing. Actual size about one-fourth of an inch.

bleeding, and cramps may be more severe. Many women have miscarriages at this stage without ever knowing it. Their period may begin slowly, with spotting over several days. It may come on time or up to three weeks late. Going through it is as physically unpleasant as a very heavy period can be. Even earlier miscarriages, called "occult," can occur before the embryo implants in the wall of the uterus. When these occur a woman will have a completely normal period, without any delay .

For women who do not feel pregnant and are not aware that they are pregnant, it is as if they have not had a miscarriage. But some women know they are pregnant even within a few days after conception. Others are watching for signs of pregnancy and

FIGURE 3. Human embryo at 6 weeks after fertilization (about 8 weeks of pregnancy). This embryo/fetus can be clearly made-out by ultrasound, and measured. Its main feature in ultrasound is a beating heart. The gills are developing into inside structures: parts of the jaw, throat and ears. The primitive reproductive system is forming and looks the same in males and females. Actual size about one-half to three-fourths of an inch.

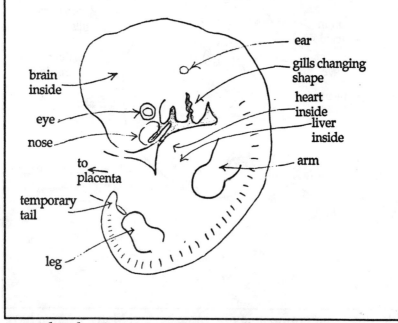

may take a home pregnancy test, usually a day or two after their period is due. For these women, if the miscarriage begins slowly, it can be very confusing. Most obstetricians will assure them that many women spot during pregnancy. Some women are told that spotting is normal in early pregnancy after the embryo implants in the uterus. Early pregnancy spotting causes an uncertainty that is harder to deal with than the physical discomfort.

> I didn't know what was normal. I didn't know what to expect. Am I miscarrying or not? My doctor didn't even want to see me. "Don't worry, it will be fine." It took me a while to figure out what was happening.

FIGURE 4. Human fetus at 8 weeks after fertilization (about 10 weeks of pregnancy). The reproductive system is shaping into specifically male or female form. The basic structure of all organ systems has formed. Actual size about one inch.

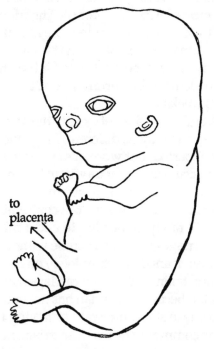

to placenta

For some women the early miscarriage may be the first news of the pregnancy.

I found out I was pregnant right when I was miscarrying. I wasn't aware that my period was late, because I have always had extremely irregular periods. At that point I wasn't charting things, but we had been trying for a couple of years. I was working and I suddenly started feeling these pains in my abdomen. I was in intense pain and I didn't know why. I went to the doctor and he did a pregnancy test and told me I was miscarrying. It was bizarre. When I found out I was pregnant I was elated, but my doctor was not smiling. And indeed I did miscarry.

In some cases a woman will be seen by her obstetrician when she starts spotting. But most clinicians will not take any action this early in pregnancy. A standard pregnancy test will probably be positive during the time of spotting, because even if the embryo has died, the young placenta will still be releasing the pregnancy hormone HCG (chapter 6). The uterus is still very small. When ultrasound is performed, the age of the embryo or fetus is always estimated plus-or-minus two weeks. The embryo in its gestation sac can just be made out for the first time around 6 weeks. It is difficult to be certain about the condition of an embryo before 8 weeks.

All "6-week embryos" are not exactly the same size. Their actual day of conception may be different. Pregnancy is dated from the last menstrual period, but women's cycles vary from 21 to 40 days. Ovulation occurs on about day 10 in the shortest cycle and about day 26 in the longest. This means there can be more than 2 weeks' difference in the true age of "6-week" embryos.

A D and C will rarely be needed to end a miscarriage at 4-7 weeks. The miscarriage can run its course without medical treatment. The uterus is cleaned out completely on its own, and blood loss is not life-threatening. Many miscarriages occur at this stage and are unreported because a woman has not had a clinical pregnancy test, or because she is unaware of having miscarried. For these reasons the commonly heard miscarriage rate of 20 percent greatly underestimates the actual frequency of miscarriage.

Sometimes an embryo will stop developing between 4 and 7 weeks, but the pregnancy will not terminate. A miscarriage has occurred, but it is not apparent. This is called a "missed" miscarriage. There may be no signs at all, or there may be spotting. The spotting may continue or stop. The obvious events we associate with miscarriage—bleeding, contractions, and the loss of fetal tissues—may be delayed for several weeks.

One unfortunate variation on an early miscarriage that may occur at this early time is called an ectopic pregnancy. *Ecto* is Greek for "outside." The egg is released to the uterine tube, and conception occurs. But though the tiny sperm made it to the egg, the much larger, egg-sized embryo cannot get through the uterine tube to the uterus. The uterine tube cannot support a pregnancy. There will be pain and bleeding, which may be mistaken for a period or for miscarriage of an embryo in the uterus. Ectopic pregnancy is a kind of miscarriage, but it is more life-threatening. It must be surgically removed under general anesthesia, and the tube may be too damaged to function again. Only about 1 percent of pregnancies are ectopic, though some women are at greater risk than others because of damaged or anatomically abnormal tubes.

The majority of detected miscarriages occur between 8 and 12 weeks. When a genetically abnormal embryo is formed, it rarely lives past 12 weeks. A miscarriage that occurs at this time may or may not require medical treatment. This will depend on the practices of a woman's obstetrician and the amount of pain and bleeding she is experiencing. It will also depend on the degree of certainty that she is miscarrying.

> At about 8 weeks I had some bleeding, then spotting and cramping for the rest of that month. Towards the end the cramping was more severe. I was very concerned, but since this was my first pregnancy, I had nothing to compare my experience to, so I thought it was just normal.

Miscarriage almost always begins with spotting. Of course, as many women have heard, "it is not uncommon for women to spot during pregnancy," so spotting is not an absolute sign that a miscarriage will occur. According to clinical records, the majority of pregnancies with reported spotting do not end in miscarriage. There are no absolute rules, and even if a woman has had several pregnancies, her doctor may not be able to see a pattern. Of the women I interviewed, about half had had at least one successful pregnancy with spotting; the others had never had spotting during their pregnancies to term.

Spotting, with or without cramps, is called a "threatened" miscarriage. It may stop after a few days, or lead to miscarriage. The miscarriage may occur within a 24-hour period, or take more than a week. Some miscarriages happen so fast that a woman will not have time to be seen by her doctor before the spotting proceeds to uterine contractions and heavy bleeding.

If a miscarriage at 8-12 weeks starts slowly, with only spotting for a few days, a woman will often be in contact with her obstetrician and may be examined. Some doctors perform a pelvic exam to see if her cervix is closed. Other doctors consider a pelvic exam risky during a threatened miscarriage. Next, the doctor feels the size of her uterus. If her cervix is closed and her uterus is the size expected for the length of her pregnancy, many doctors will advise that she do nothing but rest and wait for the spotting to stop. If a woman is 12 weeks pregnant, the fetal heartbeat can be checked externally. If everything looks normal, the doctor will advise that the woman rest at home. If the cervix is open, there is a strong chance that a woman will miscarry. This is called an "inevitable" miscarriage. If her cervix is open and there is no fetal heartbeat and no fetus seen by ultrasound, then her miscarriage is underway.

Many women who threaten miscarriage do not miscarry. They go on to deliver a normal baby at term. The temporary bleeding may be due to weakness of the placenta or the cervix, to infection, to lowered hormone levels, or other causes. The bleeding may be coming from a part of the uterus that is far away from the site of implantation. As long as the embryo is healthy, it has a chance of making it to term. Relieving physical stress by resting can help the pregnancy cure itself when the problem is not extreme.

Most doctors recommend that women curtail their physical activity, preferably by lying down, while spotting. If bleeding becomes heavy, they should come in to be examined. If the embryo is not living, lying down just calms the woman and allows her to rest but does not influence the outcome of the pregnancy. If the embryo is alive and normal, resting might help. But if there are serious physical problems with the uterus, inadequate hormones, or an infection, lying down will often not be enough. Physicians who advise rest without examining the woman are betting on the odds that it has already been determined whether the pregnancy will succeed or fail and that there is no way to influence the outcome. We will discuss the causes and treatments of miscarriage in part III.

Some medical groups include ultrasound as a routine procedure during pregnancy exams, but many do not. Routine ultrasound is done to see that the embryo is developing on schedule. It is often used to predict a due date, estimating the age of the embryo from its size. If ultrasound is performed between 8 and 12 weeks, it is very clear to the obstetrician whether or not a normal fetus is there. A normal fetus is about an inch long at this stage, with a prominent head and beating heart. The beating heart, "fetal cardiac motion," is the surest sign of a normal pregnancy. If it is not observed, the obstetrician is certain of fetal death.

The watery balloon that surrounds the fetus is called the "amniotic sac" or "gestation sac." Starting at about 8 weeks of pregnancy, the amniotic sac and the fetus can be "seen" with ultrasound. The ultrasound images are called "echoes," because they are made from sound waves that bounce off solid structures. The images are created by computer interpretation of sound bouncing patterns. The most informative ultrasound technique is called "real time imaging," and great detail and motion can be observed.

The main ultrasound results indicating a miscarriage are images of an empty amniotic sac about an inch across. An empty sac of this size shows that a pregnancy had begun but the embryo never developed, or died very early. Usually this is called simply, "the empty sac," but some obstetricians still use the term "blighted ovum." Blighted ovum is an unfortunate, insensitive term. It is archaic—blighted is a rarely used word—and a misnomer. A blighted ovum is not really an ovum, which is an egg, but an embryo that died very early in development. However, blighted ovum is a proper medical term. The embryo and its newly formed sac are referred to as "the ovum" for the first week of development, until implantation begins. This is because of the name used from the moment of ovulation, and refers to the unattached, free-floating state, whether egg or embryo.

The term blighted ovum is used when the amniotic sac is detected with ultrasound and is about an inch across, but has no fetal echoes. Obstetricians using this term do not understand the impact it has on women who have become excited about their pregnancy.

> What I had was termed a blighted ovum. It never really developed. It was not a formed baby that I lost. It was an in-between thing. I felt pregnant, just as I had with my first baby. I felt all the symptoms, all the excitement. But a blighted ovum. It made me feel bad, like I wasn't really pregnant. So when I miscarried, it wasn't a real miscarriage. I didn't really lose anything. That was an awkward feeling. I didn't know how to deal with it.

Some women who have not had any spotting go in for a routine pregnancy exam, and ultrasound detects an empty sac, revealing a missed miscarriage. When ultrasound shows there is no living fetus, the obstetrician will tell a woman she is miscarrying. At this point some doctors will offer to do a D and C. This option requires great trust in the ultrasound results, because a woman may feel quite pregnant, and have no personal evidence that she is not. Many doctors will not do a D and C in these cases. If the pregnancy is not accurately dated, a woman may be carrying a younger embryo than expected. These earlier embryos may look like the empty sac on ultrasound, though the gestation sac will be smaller than an inch in diameter.

Whether the doctor or the woman herself makes the decision, the result is that she will go on as before, waiting for something to happen. This woman was pregnant for the first time:

> I went to the doctor at 9 weeks and he did an ultrasound and couldn't find a heartbeat. All of a sudden everyone was bustling around the office and they were all worried. The doctor said it was a blighted ovum. He said I was going to have a miscarriage, but he didn't want to do any procedures. I didn't really believe him. I was holding on to see if maybe it was going to be okay. In one way I knew, and in another I thought, "But I'm still pregnant." I didn't finally miscarry until about 12 weeks. My pregnancy symptoms did not go away during that time.

The ultrasound image of an empty sac, or early embryo without a beating heart, is generally considered evidence that the embryo that initially formed was abnormal. As we will see later, chromosomal defects are most often the cause of these early miscarriages. A sequence of events that is more difficult to explain is miscarriage after seeing a normal fetus on ultrasound.

After an embryo or fetus stops developing, it can take 1-6 weeks for the miscarriage to continue to completion.

> Around six weeks I noticed some pinkish color. My doctor told me not to worry about it, but to come in and he would do an ultrasound. Nothing showed up; there was no heartbeat. I had a positive pregnancy test. I had all the symptoms of being pregnant. I went in every week to have ultrasound. It was very expensive. The fetus was developing slightly, but there was no heartbeat. And then it stopped developing. They kept doing the blood test. I kept showing symptoms of pregnancy. About nine weeks they concluded that the fetus was dead. We waited two more weeks, then my doctor set me up for a D and C. The day before it was scheduled I bled spontaneously. I went to the hospital and they performed the D and C. I had very mild cramps. It almost seemed like nothing happened. The hardest part of it all was the waiting. I kept hoping, every time I went to the doctor, that there would be a heartbeat, that it would be a viable pregnancy.

The usual course of events after embryo death is for bleeding to start in the part of the uterus attached to the placenta (decidua basalis). The bleeding causes local tissue damage and inflammation, which is an invasion of white blood cells. Next the gestation sac, with or without an embryo, separates from the placenta. This stimulates uterine contractions, as if the gestation sac were a foreign body. Then the cervix begins to dilate. Finally the gestation sac is expelled, followed by the placenta and uterine tissue (decidua) over several days of bleeding (figure 5).

Waiting for a miscarriage is agonizing, but it is often better than waiting in uncertainty. The ultrasound news is heartbreaking, but for many women it gives them time to accept something that would otherwise take them by surprise during the physical trauma itself. The fore-knowledge allows the separation of the

FIGURE 5. Diagram of the course of miscarriage. These figures show miscarriage at about 10 weeks. In A) the early placenta is expelled with the fetus and gestation sac. In B) part or all of the placenta remains in the uterus, causing continued contractions and bleeding.

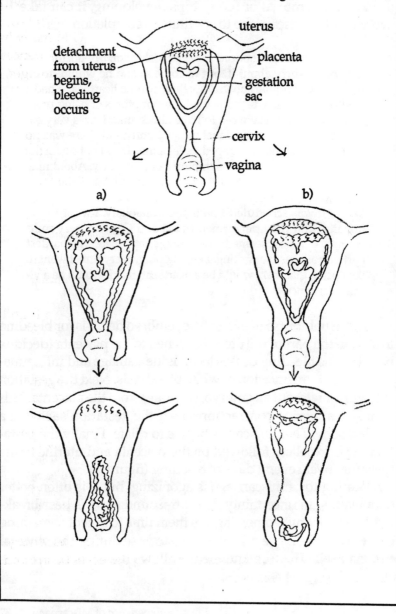

emotional loss from the physical fright. Also, when the miscarriage does happen, it is expected and certain, and the woman is spared feelings of blind fear: "What is happening to me?"

Whether she is examined by her doctor or not, when a woman finally miscarries between 8 and 12 weeks, she will know it. Most often she will have heavy bleeding, with large clots. She will usually have cramps, but they can vary greatly in severity. She may deliver a dead fetus. Any of these experiences can be quite scary, and enough to send a woman to the emergency room. One woman had a miscarriage at 9 weeks:

> The pain was minor. I have had more painful periods. But when I saw the blood I was overwhelmed. I called the doctor. His nurse said to go to bed, so I did. The cramping and bleeding became more intense. I was scared. I felt abnormal, unnatural. My husband insisted we go to the doctor. It was about 11 at night. We bundled up our sleeping 3-year-old and went to emergency. They were pretty nice, but I was insulted when the nurse asked if I had had a positive pregnancy test. When the doctor examined me, the fetal tissue plopped right into his hand.
>
> He said, "Yes, you've had a miscarriage." I felt they had been doubting me all along. I was sent home without further treatment.

A woman and her doctor must decide whether to have a D and C or wait for nature to take its course.

> At about 8 weeks I started bleeding heavily. I bled for about two days, off and on. My doctor said to stay in bed, so I stayed in bed, but I kept bleeding. Then my doctor examined me and said my uterus was small. She sent me to another doctor for ultrasound. I was very anxious. He said that the tissues were moving toward the mouth of the cervix. Then my doctor said she could send me to have the D and C now, or we could wait a few days. I did not want to wait. I wanted it to be done. I wanted to go home and have whatever had been a baby, that was now dead, out of me. The D and C hurt quite a bit for a short time, but it was not overwhelming.

Sometimes spotting can be very long-term, but the miscarriage abrupt. One woman had almost identical experiences before and after her first child was born:

I had spotting and cramps starting at 8 weeks. Then one evening, at 12 weeks, the cramping became worse. I felt a strong pressure on my abdomen. I went to the toilet and within a few minutes the fetus was pushed out. I sat there for several minutes, taking fleeting glances at it, and feeling very numb. I went to the doctor and I was already dilated. He took out some of the placenta, but there was still a lot left, so I had bleeding and cramping for a couple of weeks. The doctor checked me two weeks later to be sure I was okay.

The following year I had a successful pregnancy. I did have spotting, but it was not as heavy. The doctor said "Don't worry, this can happen. People can have heavy bleeding, and still give birth at term." It never got that heavy, and then went away.

In my third pregnancy I had spotting and cramps starting at 6 weeks. I felt certain I was going to miscarry. I found myself thinking, "If it's going to happen, I wish it would happen now, and not drag out for a whole month." But it did continue. Then one day, at 11 weeks, I was resting in bed, the cramping increased and a pressure in my uterus started building up. I went into the bathroom, sat on the toilet, and out came the baby. It was not a shock this time. I even looked for quite awhile at the tiny little body floating in the toilet bowl. I had quite a bit of heavy bleeding this time. I had a D and C, which was painful and depressing, but afterwards I felt relieved. I had no more cramping or bleeding.

Bleeding during the actual miscarriage is also variable. Some women spot for a few days, then suddenly gush. Others begin by spotting, then the flow gradually increases day by day, until it is quite heavy. At the late stage the most frightening thing for many women is the huge clots they produce. Where can they all be coming from, and when will they stop? One woman's first pregnancy ended at 12 weeks:

I spent all night cramping. I sort of knew I was miscarrying, but I wasn't sure. I didn't get any sleep. I had to get up in the morning to put on a brunch. I wore something vaguely presentable. The people stayed and stayed. I was feeling awful: tired and sick, having cramps, and here I was serving brunch. I didn't want anybody to think anything was really wrong. "I can bear up to it. Everyone has a baby. Just because I'm pregnant doesn't mean....." Finally, after several hours, they left. I cleared out the dishes, cleaned everything up. I climbed up the ladder to the loft bed, took a magazine, and lay down. Suddenly everything gushed out all over. I raced down the ladder, leaving pools of blood on the way to the bathroom. And these huge clots, the size of my fist. They were scary.

Sometimes bleeding is no heavier than a bad period, with no clots. Some women deliver a fetus, often with slight bleeding. Many never see anything resembling human tissue. Cramps, which are uterine contractions, are almost universal at this stage. They also can vary in intensity. Women who have gone through childbirth will find them much more tolerable than women who have not. They usually begin feeling like menstrual cramps, and then get more and more intense. In one woman's second miscarriage:

> I was 11 weeks and spotted for a week and a half before the miscarriage actually took place. I stayed home from work all week. I didn't tell anyone. I was going to stick it out, do it by myself. I didn't want to have to deal with the hospital. But I didn't realize that at 11 weeks your body really goes into labor. The first night I thought, "This is not very much fun, but it's not too bad." The next day it got worse and worse. I was lying there in my bedroom all by myself and I could hardly talk. I called my friends at work and said, "Help, come get me, I'm having a miscarriage." One of my friends came and took me to the hospital. And my doctor was in surgery, so they couldn't give me anything for pain. I cried, "There's no reason for me to go through all this pain. I'm not even having a baby!"

If a woman stays home for the miscarriage, her obstetrician will want to examine her within a couple of weeks to check the size of her uterus manually. Some order ultrasound to be sure that the uterus is clear of remaining tissue. If it is clean, the miscarriage is "complete." If tissue remains in the uterus, the miscarriage is incomplete, and the doctor will recommend a D and C. There is great risk with an incomplete miscarriage. Excessive loss of blood can lead to shock. Remaining tissue in the uterus can cause serious infection.

Up until 12 weeks, before the placenta is fully developed,

miscarriages often complete themselves safely without medical intervention. After 12 weeks, the gestation sac is often retained with the placenta while the fetus is expelled (see figure 5). The placenta is more developed and yet not easily shed by the uterus, as it is at birth. A miscarriage that occurs between 12 and 20 weeks is almost certain to require medical treatment, usually a D and E (evacuation, cleaning out the uterus by suction), to be sure that all fetal and placental tissue is removed from the uterus.

There is still variation in the course of the miscarriage at this stage. After an embryo dies, it takes time for hormone signals to stop coming from it to the placenta or the ovaries (chapter 7). Thus there is a lag time before the tissues are rejected by the uterus. If the embryo and placenta were quite small when they stopped growing, there can be less effort on the part of the uterus to expel them, and they will come out as a unit. Thus a late miscarriage will be experienced physically as an early one.

In other cases a normal fetus dies because of premature labor caused by failure of the placenta, malformation of the uterus, or an infection. Some late miscarriages are due to a weak cervix, a condition called "cervical incompetence." The pressure from the uterus causes the cervix to give way without much effort. Miscarriage due to incompetent cervix may be fairly painless. Late miscarriages due to early labor will violently remove the fully grown fetus from the uterus, resulting in fetal death. The fetus is often separated from the placenta, which can be partly retained in the uterus: an incomplete miscarriage. Thus, some late miscarriages are quite painful and bloody. Sometimes women are given labor-inducing hormones, such as oxytocin (Pitocin) or prostaglandins, to stimulate uterine contractions and help remove the placental tissue, completing the miscarriage.

> I was almost 5 months pregnant. I had a routine exam, and my doctor said he was having a hard time locating the heartbeat, but not to get excited, he would check with ultrasound. There was no heartbeat or movement of any kind. They sent me home and told me my body would take over soon. The cramps began on Christmas eve. They were real strong, like birth labor. Then I started bleeding and expelling tissue. I went to the hospital and

they gave me intravenous Pitocin. Early Christmas morning they did a D and E.

Late miscarriage is much more painful and frightening for a woman who has never had a baby, because she has not been prepared to deal with strong uterine contractions. A woman who has given birth has very often taken childbirth classes to learn breathing techniques, and can handle contractions fairly well. As with all miscarriages, once a D and C or D and E is performed, the pain stops.

Whether the pain is intense or mild, whether it occurs suddenly or is drawn-out, a miscarriage is a physical shock. What should a woman do if she starts spotting during a pregnancy? If she is at least 8 weeks pregnant, her best course is to request ultrasound. Then she will know whether she should fight to save a living fetus. If a woman has had a miscarriage before, she is often determined to do something, not sit helplessly by, waiting to see what nature will do. When spotting starts she may pressure her doctor to prescribe hormone supplements. If the pregnancy succeeds, it cannot be proven that the hormones were necessary. Some women accept the advice of their obstetrician: "You cannot do anything, what will happen will happen. This is a normal function of your body. Let's just wait and see." We will see in Part III that some causes of miscarriage are preventable by intervention, while others are not.

Chapter 3

Coping with the Emotions of A Miscarriage

AFTER SURVIVING THE UNCERTAINTY, PAIN, AND FEAR of miscarriage, a woman faces a longer, more difficult time, the emotional aftermath. This is a time of grief for a child that will never be born. It is a time of feeling cast adrift, cut off from others by emotions no one else understands. It is a time when a woman feels she is a failure, when she may have doubts about her future as a mother. It is a time of spoiled plans and of disappointment. A woman needs to take some time to heal and feel connected with others again. In this chapter I will discuss the range of emotions women experience after a miscarriage and the efforts they make to get through these painful feelings. In addition, I will describe women's reactions to the responses of mates, doctors, friends and relatives, and feelings about being pregnant again. I will discuss the kinds of feelings that are normal at this time and give some advice on finding solace and support.

The message I hope to convey to women who have miscarried is that many other women are having the same feelings as you. You are not a failure. It is all right to feel sad. You will feel better in time. As in chapter 2, this chapter draws on stories women have shared with me. The sharing of these experiences is excellent therapy. It feels safe to talk about your feelings with someone who has had a similar experience. It is uplifting to find that another person feels as you do when you have been feeling alone, even freakish. This chapter also draws on discussions I have had with mental health professionals and on reports in medical journals.

Part A: First Emotions

There are many words women use to describe how they feel after a miscarriage. Certain emotions are mentioned by almost everyone. A sense of failure and some level of grief are the most common. Variations on these, as well as disappointment and isolation are often expressed. For women who have never had children there is a special worry over their ability to have a child. These and related feelings are very normal.

During the miscarriage itself, a very strong feeling of being alone is often reported. This is part of the unexpected nature of the miscarriage, the fear and uncertainty about what is happening. The aloneness also stems from a sense of doing something wrong: a woman was supposed to carry a baby to term, and celebrate childbirth. Instead she failed. She and her husband had decided it was time to have a baby. They went through the fun, effort, and anticipation of getting pregnant. For some couples this took a month, for others more than a year. Now a baby was on the way. Suddenly, spotting started. It had taken two people to get pregnant, but only one to mess up their plans. The woman became an observer of her own body, watching helplessly from the sidelines while the baby was lost. This was not what she had read about in her pregnancy books.

While going through a miscarriage, many women feel the need to act as if nothing is happening. Maybe they can stop it by will power. There is often a need to be tough. They are losing control of their bodies; they try to retain control of their emotions. One woman miscarried on the day of a family wedding and found herself being "very cheerful, almost too cheerful," all day. This was to fend off the "double whammy" of losing emotional control at the same time as losing control of her body. Another woman went through five weeks of ultrasound checks after brief spotting, gradually learning that her pregnancy would not succeed:

> I like to be in control of everything that goes on in my life, and I'm very exacting. While I was going through it I tried to think how I could fix it. What could I do: walk slowly, or lie down? How could

I make this baby live and not die? I felt very awkward, as if I had
absolutely no control.

A feeling of aloneness stays with many women after the
physical fright is over. Now it relates to a complex net of feelings
including grief, guilt, and worry. She feels sad, but has a sense that
she has no right to any sympathy or help. She messed up a normal
function; she is incompetent. She is different from everyone else.
She did not suffer a loss—she wasn't even showing yet.

She has never heard of a support group for women who miscarry. These are rare, and not publicized. Some hospitals have
one support group for all kinds of loss: miscarriage, stillbirth,
and death of a newborn. Psychotherapists have learned that the
feelings of grief are the same for all three losses and feel that any
woman can benefit from talking or listening to such a group. But
most of the women I interviewed said they would only feel com-
fortable in a group exclusively for miscarriage. While it is gratify-
ing to know that the loss of miscarriage is now considered to
weigh as heavily as stillbirth or death of a newborn, women who
miscarry still feel they are in a different league. For some women
it is too much to consider worse possibilities than the miscarriage. Others assume that the women in the group will not see
that their problem is worthy of the same sympathy.

It is unfortunate that a woman should have to feel alone
when there are so many other women who have miscarried, who
can listen to her grief, share their sympathy and understanding,
and let her know she is normal.

> I wish I had grown up with the knowledge that one out of four
> pregnancies ends in miscarriage. Most women I know who had
> miscarriages never heard that before. That kind of information is
> what we need. Instead all we know is: you get pregnant, you
> have a baby. If you have a miscarriage, there is something wrong
> with you.

The feeling of failure is one of the most universal of emotions
after a miscarriage. It is expressed in various ways:

> I felt I was incompetent. Of course I heard what the doctor said.

The doctor said there was something wrong with the embryo, so it should not have gone to term, and that was how the body took care of that. And I believed that. But I still felt incompetent.

Or:

I had been responsible for that child, and I let it down. In my prayers I apologized to it. Then I had a second miscarriage when my daughter was 18 months old. It was not as devastating because I was very thankful for her. Yet I still had an overwhelming feeling of not living up to my responsibilities as a mother. I had failed at keeping that baby alive and healthy inside my womb.

This feeling may include a sense of failing one's husband and family, everyone who had been counting on her to produce a child. "I was not prepared for it emotionally. I was very disappointed, because we were looking forward to the pregnancy and had begun to tell the family. I felt as though I let everybody down."

There is an intimate association between a pregnant woman's body and her baby. Unlike a separate person who dies, this baby existed only as an internal part of the woman. The sense of failure becomes shame, and makes it difficult for a woman to properly mourn the baby that was not to be. The victim is also the perpetrator. Everyone asks, what went wrong? The woman asks herself: What did I do wrong? The failed feeling can take the form of guilt for having caused the miscarriage. Many women feel they did not take proper care of their bodies. Some real or imagined abuse might have occurred long before the pregnancy. Any number of explanations will be considered. "I searched for every possible reason: Was I a DES baby? Was my husband's prior drug use to blame? Wasn't I being careful enough? I wanted to understand. I was very frustrated."

Many women feel there must be some direct connection with their recent behavior. "I was working at the time and thought maybe I'd overdone it, and I had run about a half a block right before the initial bleeding started." Similarly:

Several days before I started spotting I had a dream that I miscarried, and when it really happened, I was shocked and felt that I might have done something that contributed. I was on-call in my residency training program the day before.

Others mix any reasons they can find to take the blame:

> My doctor said it was for the best. There was probably some defect that was too gross for it to develop into a baby. I began to feel guilty because I had had extensive X-rays to my lower back, for a workman's compensation case. I thought I really screwed up. My eggs are all nuked. And I hadn't even been sure that I wanted to get pregnant at the time. But I was thirty-two and beginning to feel the pressure. After I became pregnant I was ambivalent about it. Then I felt that my ambivalence had caused the miscarriage. I am still pretty certain that's a contributing factor.

There are endless ways to rationalize a miscarriage. Often women think of some reason why they were meant to have a miscarriage: The first child wasn't old enough. The husband wasn't ready. They weren't sure. And so on. Women who had therapeutic abortions ten or even twenty years earlier tell themselves that must be why they miscarried. This may come partly from guilt about the abortion, but primarily it is a search for balance. It stems from a need to fit the miscarriage into some worldly order. This way a woman can accept it as a natural episode in her life. Of course, no woman is ever meant to have a miscarriage.

Sometimes miscarriage ends an unwanted pregnancy. This can be a relief, but is very often more difficult to deal with than having an elective abortion. This woman had a second miscarriage after having two healthy children, with her first miscarriage in between them.

> The second one was more traumatic. I don't know why. It was unplanned, and it happened much sooner. I got much sicker emotionally; I had a big depression afterwards. We had not yet decided not to have more kids. I thought one more might be nice, but we hadn't planned this, and I was waiting for more time, for my daughter to get older, and for things to be happier. I had planned fairly soon—80 percent of me said I was going to abort this. Actually I had scheduled it for a week later, but then I started miscarrying. I was relieved when I saw the spotting, but then I fell

apart. From that point on I was in another world emotionally. I felt like I was grieving for somebody who had died, but I felt like it was myself who had died.

Another expression of failure is a feeling of embarrassment. As one woman put it, "The worst part is un-telling everyone. 'Oh, by the way, I'm *not* pregnant. Scratch it. I'll let you know.'" And another said, " I had told everyone the moment I got pregnant, because it was an exciting new thing that we were doing. I was really really embarrassed, having to go and tell everybody, 'Oh, I had a miscarriage.'" This embarrassment is due to a woman's feeling of shame or inadequacy; a loss of trust in herself. It is as if she was not really pregnant, and had misled her family and friends. Many women who have miscarried do not tell people when they get pregnant again. They do not want to have to tell people if they miscarry again. And it is hard to believe in the next pregnancy. After all, no one but a woman and her doctor has any evidence that she is really pregnant until she is "big with child."

> We did not tell more than four people as opposed to twenty or more the first time. I didn't even tell my sister. If I miscarried again I did not want to have to tell all those people. It would be too painful. I didn't want to talk to them again about my feelings of incompetence.

Women often say that the miscarriage makes them feel they have no control over their body. "I felt out of control. I'm used to being in charge of my life. I had decided to have a baby, and I thought the decision was the hurdle, not having the baby!" Also, as one therapist puts it,

> People of our generation are very organized; they plan things. By the time a woman reaches her ninth or tenth week, she's got her life planned out: her career, her vacation, and so on. She thought by June of 1990 she would be sitting at home taking care of a baby, but all of a sudden that's not going to happen. It impacts every part of her life, just as a child would have. There is a feeling of despair and emptiness. She has to come back to reality.

Another woman put it this way: "Suddenly it's all out of our hands; our planning and foresight are for nought. It is not just planning for the baby, but our whole way of living that is challenged."

When miscarriage occurs, many women are already strongly attached to their expected baby. Others may not yet have formed an emotional bond. Some women get pregnant accidentally and are ambivalent about having a child. This range of emotional investment in the pregnancy gives a range of feelings of loss after a miscarriage. Women who have attached to their anticipated baby feel very sad about its death. This sadness can be quite intense, and it helps to face it. One woman relates,

> The most loving and welcome comment I heard was from someone who said, "Most people don't realize it but you have just experienced a great loss and must go through a period of grieving and acceptance before feeling better." It felt good to have someone acknowledge the magnitude of my sadness.

A woman has lost an anticipated child. She is mourning her loss. But it is not always recognized as real by her husband, her family, or friends. It is difficult to find a way to express and deal with her feelings. Some women are plunged into deep sorrow. Others experience a vague depression. Many feel cut off from everyone by their strong emotions. One woman miscarried twice, both times at 12 weeks:

> Everybody means well, but they try to make light of it. They try to be cheery about it. The word "grieve" doesn't seem to apply to miscarriages. People don't make the connection. But it was a life. I still find myself wondering what those babies would be like. I wonder in a spiritual sense, where are they in the cosmos?

Even though a woman has not seen her baby or held it in her arms, she has given it a life in her mind. One woman's first pregnancy ended at 6 weeks:

> I was surprised at how devastating it was—I had already bonded to this baby and found that everything around me reminded me of

my lost baby. I resented pregnant women and women with children. I couldn't stop crying. It was unbearable grief.

Another had a miscarriage between children, at 9 weeks.

A miscarriage is so private and personal. It is a lonely experience because you don't look pregnant, so you are the only one truly aware of the changes. Once the attachment is made to the baby, the loss is extremely painful. All your hopes, dreams, and fantasies vanish.

What does it mean to say a woman has attached to an expected baby? It means she has already started to love this child. It does not matter whether she believes this is yet a legal human life; it is her picture of the child that will be born in six or seven or eight months. And then it is not to be born. The love that had started to flow must be stopped. Women who already have one or more children often take comfort in them and feel grateful for them. Each child provides "a place where she can pour out all that love, and the child acts as a buffer and keeps her from feeling completely failed."

Even so, there will be grief for the lost love. Human grief has been studied extensively by physicians and psychologists. It can be helpful to know that most people who lose loved ones are found to pass through a series of emotional stages over several months, even a couple of years. There have not been scientific studies of the mourning process after miscarriage alone, but in larger studies women report the same kinds of emotions after miscarriage as after stillbirth or loss of a newborn.

The majority of women who miscarry do not see their dead fetus. As we saw in chapter 2, many miscarriages occur some time after a small, poorly formed embryo has died. In some cases though, especially in later miscarriages, a whole fetus is delivered before a woman gets to her doctor. Seeing the little figure is usually a shock. This shock can be experienced as a feeling of numbness or detachment. Some women are able to look over the dead fetus out of curiosity. Others think to say good-bye. After the miscarriage is over, women who have seen the dead fetus seem to be very clear about their sadness and to indulge in a strong, very focused act of mourning. Although they are not spared from feelings of failure and guilt, they seem to have an easier time knowing their sadness was for someone who had really been there. Not seeing the lost baby makes it harder to get in touch with one's grief. A woman is not sure why she feels so bad. Her self-doubt may be worse, because many of her bad feelings, which are really sadness over the baby, are misdirected at herself and her sense of failure.

> I kept questioning whether this was a real pregnancy. Should I treat it as a death or not? Finally I came to the conclusion that it was. You are made to feel like it is not okay to miscarry, and not okay to feel as if you have lost anything because there was not anything there. Other friends have miscarried, and there was actually a body there that they could autopsy, figure out why. In my case there was nothing, just scrapings. That was really hard. That is always in the back of my mind, that it wasn't a true miscarriage.

Until about fifteen years ago, women who had stillborn babies, or whose infants died soon after birth, were "protected" from the trauma of seeing them. Now it has become accepted throughout the medical community that seeing a lost baby and saying good-bye helps a woman, and her husband, to start the mourning process. Grief is a term that refers to a family of emotions associated with losing a loved one, such as sadness, guilt, anger, shame, and anxiety. Mourning is the process of working through these emotions. Mourning is everything a person does to resolve, or learn to live with, a loss.

Many psychological and physical problems are thought to arise from grief and to linger in people who have not been able to really mourn. If seeing and remembering a lost baby helps a woman get in touch with her grief, then women who have not seen their miscarried babies will have a harder time. This is not to say that mourning is easy. But when a woman acknowledges her sadness, even setting aside time to express her sorrow, she can finally accept it, and fit it in with her life, instead of having it take over her life. It is much harder when all her bad feelings are turned on herself.

> I was really depressed. A lot of things were happening medically to me; my whole body was being treated for this, what they termed as not really a viable pregnancy. I was given general anesthesia; I was in the hospital overnight, which was very expensive. That made me even more depressed. I had never been away from my son overnight. It really affected our lives. I came home and I didn't feel like doing anything. I felt guilty, embarrassed, sad, like it was a waste. It took me a long time to recoup from that. After a few months I did a ritual called the mikvah. I went to the mikvah to get cleansed, renew my body. In this ritual you go under the water, go through the rebirth process. We sang songs, and I cried. It was a way of—not ending it—but acknowledging the baby that had died. That helped a lot.

Depending on the individual, the extent of her dreaming and planning for the baby, each part of her mourning process can vary. Anger, guilt, sadness, and other feelings each come and go, and change in focus and strength, over time. It helps to realize that these feelings can surface any time. It helps for a woman to talk to her husband and ask him to understand that her up-and-down emotions are normal and can last for months. If she can accept these feelings, she will begin to feel better.

Part B: Support

Women who have miscarriages need to find support and understanding from their mates, friends, and family. "My two best friends dropped everything when they found out how sad I was, and came to console me." "My friends were very understanding of my feelings of loss, and they pointed out that many of their friends had miscarriages followed by normal pregnancies." "My obstetrician was very supportive and reassuring."

> I had two friends who were pregnant, and we were all due at the same time. It was really hard for me to watch my friends continue with their pregnancies. One of the women who gave me the most

support was pregnant. I felt really bad, because I didn't want my
bad luck to rub off on her. It was an awkward situation. I had
wanted all our babies to be born at the same time, and to all be
friends. And I kept feeling bad for them knowing that they knew
I had miscarried, and what were they feeling for me.

Women often report that their husbands are supportive
during and after the miscarriage. Some men take off a day or two
from work to help their wives recover. Many men offer en-
couragement echoing the doctor's assurance that they will try
again and will surely be able to have a baby. It is common for
men to be more worried about their wife's suffering than the loss
of the baby. However, some men are deeply saddened by the
loss, since a baby can have a life in a man's mind, too. Often the
husband does not speak about the baby until his wife presses
him. This may be his way of handling grief. It may involve a
need to avoid his wife's strong emotions. Still other men are just
not very deeply involved. They had not yet attached to the baby.

The most crucial thing about a husband's attitude is his
wife's perception of it, and her ability to get his support when
she needs it.

> My husband was very sensitive. During the miscarriage he was
> concerned for my health in a reassuring way. The following weeks
> he was very understanding. He knew I felt a lot worse than I acted
> or showed.

Another woman said:

> My husband was much more supportive and in control than I
> expected him to be. He was a great source of comfort. He said,
> "Don't worry, we'll try again." As time went on though, he had
> a more difficult time understanding my sadness and sense of
> loss. When I remained depressed, he was surprised that I was
> still needy.

In still another woman's view:

> The miscarriage never affected my husband as it did me. He never
> doubted our ability to have a child. He hadn't attached to the baby

as I had. I think he saw it as a chance to buy more time to prepare emotionally for a baby.

It helps a woman to get through the pain if she can talk about her feelings and sort them out. It is worth trying to talk to her husband. The miscarriage was a shared experience. The loss is a common loss. It may be the first crisis in a marriage. The more the husband and wife can talk to each other about it and help each other through the sadness, the better. A number of women I interviewed could turn to their husbands for this support, but the majority excused them. Though disappointed in their husbands' lack of concern after their recovery from the physical event, these women were not surprised by it. "It's never as real for husbands." They looked to other women for understanding and acceptance of their sorrow. It would lighten a woman's emotional burden if her husband could acknowledge and accept her grief and worries, even if he did not share these feelings or was not aware of them in himself.

> We have good communication in general, and he's a very feeling person. He really wants to be pregnant as much as I do; he really wants to be a father. We went through it together. We talked together and cried together. We have a friend who is a grief counselor, and she came over. Even though I am a therapist, it was really helpful to have her come. She didn't say anything I didn't know, but it helped to have someone else be there saying this is a death, it is appropriate to grieve and to have these kinds of feelings. My husband was ready to start trying again sooner than I was, but he respected my need to wait.

Some women do not find support in all quarters. The same words, said in different tones or contexts, can have a very different impact, depending on a woman's frame of mind. This applies to words of other family members, friends, and doctors. For one woman, "It bugged me a lot when people said, 'Oh, you can try again, it happens all the time.' Not to me!" And another felt worse when well-meaning people said, "You weren't sure you wanted a baby yet, so maybe it's for the best." One felt that "the doctor was not sympathetic. A miscarriage seemed trivial, and being upset would be a waste of time. 'It's for the best' is not what I needed to hear."

Family are not always helpful, even when they are trying to be. "My in-laws did not acknowledge the importance of the loss and did not inquire about my feelings. Instead they asked whether carrying my little boy may have contributed to the miscarriage." Sometimes intended support can be hard on a woman:

> The worst thing I remember was that my brother came over shortly after the D and C, and he hugged me tight. He was so upset for me; he was overwhelmed by my loss. I felt that I had to comfort him and be okay because he was so upset. I didn't want to have to comfort him.

A woman needs to explain the miscarriage in some way that gives her confidence to try again. This is very important if she has never had children before. If she has had one or more miscarriages before, she will want some help in preventing future ones. For some women, clear information on the causes and frequency of miscarriage will provide perspective and reassurance. An involved obstetrician can be helpful in this respect. But many are not able to spend the time or provide enough information to their patients. There is a clear connection between a woman's emotional suffering and her desire for an explanation. If the experience were confined to the loss of an unborn, untouched baby, it would be bad enough, and the grief would be deep. But added to that are many worries: Did I do something bad that made this baby die? Is something wrong with me? Will I ever be able to have a child?

Some women feel comforted when they hear, "The miscarriage was nature's way of removing an abnormal embryo. It is for the best." Others find this makes them worry more. Why was the embryo abnormal? How do I know I won't continue to make abnormal embryos? Why didn't anyone else in my family ever make an abnormal embryo? Many women's doctors will give them a stock speech on miscarriage. It can be very frustrating for someone who has miscarried a single time, because the doctor will assure her that there is no reason to worry or to pursue her

questions. If a woman really wants to know more, she will want
her doctor to answer her questions or point her to someone who
can. Parts II and III of this book are meant to answer these questions clearly.

Some women want to know what can be done to prevent a
miscarriage from happening again. Most obstetricians will not
act until a woman has several miscarriages. Unless a woman
decides to go to a fertility specialist, she will have to press her
own doctor for more attention to her next pregnancy.

Women generally feel satisfied with the medical care they
receive during the miscarriage. Afterward, their doctors assure
them they can try again to have a baby. Other women find their
doctor lacking in sympathy, and insensitive to their grief as well
as their worries. Part of this is a natural grief response of anger at
anyone associated with the miscarriage. A woman must come to
grips with her concerns and become informed enough to make
clear demands of her doctor. If she feels strongly that she did not
receive the care or sensitivity she needs, she may choose to find a
more involved obstetrician.

Many women get through their bad feelings by concentrat-
ing on living a perfect, health-conscious life and getting pregnant
again. They put all emotions and hopes on hold until they are
pregnant again. They need to prove to themselves and their
family that they can be trusted to do it right. "I was very sad. I
was depressed until I got pregnant again. So it was just waiting.
The doctor told me to wait three months before trying again."
There is no medical reason to wait through several cycles. But
many therapists suggest that "it is good to wait, because it gives
you time to mourn. There is value in having some time to let go
of your attachment to that baby." One perceptive woman related
her experience:

> I didn't want to get pregnant until I felt okay. I remember think-
> ing, I was still attached to this baby. Once after the miscarriage my
> husband made me some coffee. That sounds like a kind, loving
> thing to do. But it was caffeinated and I was hurt and furious, be-
> cause it was an acknowledgement that the baby was gone and I
> could drink caffeine. I was mad. I didn't want to drink it. I was still

holding on to that lost baby. Once I moved beyond that I was ready to get pregnant.

Some women adopt an attitude of denial. Everything is fine; it is a practical problem; we will try again. Denial is also a normal response. When they are pregnant a second time, they are suddenly faced with overwhelming emotions and find themselves constantly choking back tears. This is a roundabout way to find one's grief, and it may be uncomfortable at the time. But it is always better to face the sadness. It will slowly lose its power. When it is not acknowledged, it can continue surfacing at full force.

When a woman who has miscarried gets pregnant again, there is a natural tendency to be nervous, to resist bonding and getting excited until there is some sign that everything will be all right.

I got pregnant about four months after I miscarried. I constantly worried whether it would be a healthy pregnancy. I couldn't give my son my attention, because I was so focused on the pregnancy. I was really frightened at the thought of going through a miscarriage again. And I think I would feel the same way no matter how many times I get pregnant again. I just don't want to go through it again, and if I do, I'll feel just as bad. Each loss is a true loss.

Sometimes just getting past the time of the miscarriage helps. For most women it takes at least three months, hearing a heartbeat or seeing a growing baby on ultrasound, to become cautiously optimistic.

I just wanted to get pregnant again as soon as possible. When I did, I was extremely nervous. When I had slight bleeding I got very worried and depressed. When they couldn't get a heartbeat early on I got upset.

One woman related this experience:

I didn't discuss it much with my husband, but I worried about my ability to have kids. Even though the doctor told me not to worry, I still did. When I got pregnant again, I started bleeding at about 6 weeks. I decided that I was having a miscarriage. I felt helpless. There was nothing I could do. I called my doctor and said, "I'm having a miscarriage. I'm bleeding. It has started out just like my other two." The doctor said, "You could be having a little breakthrough bleeding, but it doesn't mean you are having a miscarriage. Just keep a watch on it and let me know." I had already given up. I was so disappointed. Then when I didn't have one I was ecstatic. I couldn't believe it. It was like rebirth.

Far fewer people are told about the next pregnancy, because it is unthinkable to have to tell them of another miscarriage.

But sometimes the next pregnancy is hard to achieve. It might have taken a long time to get pregnant the first time, and a woman wonders if it is worth the trouble again. Some women decide not to risk another pregnancy. Sometimes a woman's husband or children do not want to go through the experience of her miscarrying again, and discourage her from getting pregnant. Some women wait several years to try for a child again. "Then I didn't go to the doctor for three months. I didn't want to hear any bad news." The most important thing that these women, and all women who miscarry, can do, is to face their sadness, bid their lost child good-bye, and accept the loss. This is accomplished by private mourning and by talking to others who have miscarried. The talking also relieves women of intense feelings of incompetence and guilt and makes them feel less isolated.

It is important to acknowledge and work out the grief, disappointment, and feelings of failure even without getting pregnant again. One therapist, who also suffered a miscarriage, suggests,

> Find supportive people and talk about it. Share the experience with others who have miscarried. It is therapeutic to go over it again and again and again. You just need to get it out. And if you feel ashamed, that's what talking can do: you get less ashamed. If you can talk about it, it's okay.

Another therapist gives the following advice to a woman who has had a miscarriage:

> Take time for yourself. Acknowledge your feelings. Allow yourself to grieve. Take things at your own pace. Talk about it. Not everyone will want to hear about it, so use your judgment in finding people

you can speak to. People are hesitant to come to our support group because they don't want to expose themselves. We tell them they don't have to talk. Then they hear someone else speaking about the things they cannot articulate, and it makes them feel much more connected, more in touch with the world.

And a nonprofessional woman advises,

Let yourself go through the natural process, go through feeling the loss. Let yourself hang around the house in your pajamas, and let someone bring meals over. Let anyone who wants to, take care of you, hold your hand. Get the emotional support you need. Do not question why you are feeling the way you are. Just let yourself be, and just go through it. Involve your husband and your children as much as they can. You have to go through a catharsis.

Miscarriage is a significant tragedy in a woman's life. She has lost a tiny child. She has lost one chance at motherhood. She may feel sad, guilty, or disappointed. She may feel she has failed, or lost control of her life. If she can let these emotions surface, and talk about them with people who understand, she will begin to heal. The pain may never completely go away, but it will become a memory, lose its power over her and let her get on with her life.

Part C: Some Suggestions on How to Help Your Emotions Surface.

To mourn is to think about your sorrow, to "be in it." In cases of stillbirth and loss of a newborn, women who meet with a support group are found to take less time to resolve their loss. By sharing with the group, they get in touch with their grief and begin mourning. It is clear that this would help women who have miscarried, too. If a support group is not available, or if a woman is not inclined to participate in one, the best advice is to find another woman who has had a miscarriage. Ask friends and family, if someone does not appear. Ask about her miscarriage, and share yours with her: What was the physical experience like? Did you understand what was happening? What were your feelings while you waited, then went through the miscarriage? How did you feel afterwards? How did it feel to tell people; to go back to work? What was the hardest thing to deal with? Had your husband been excited about the pregnancy? How did he feel about the miscarriage? Did you talk about it with him? How sad were you about losing the baby? Did you cry often, or over a long time? Did thoughts of the baby come up at odd times? Did you worry about getting pregnant again? Did you try again soon? What advice would you give to a woman who has had a miscarriage?

Chapter 4

Second Miscarriage and More: A Personal Account

1987 WAS THE YEAR my fertility and resiliency were put to the test. During the year I learned that my job of eight years would be eliminated, and I got pregnant four times. Each pregnancy was physically exhausting and fraught with anxiety. I was sustained by my delightful daughter and my steady husband. In this chapter I describe my feelings during that series of three miscarriages. At the time it began I had behind me the experience of one miscarriage and one complete pregnancy and delivery. The successful pregnancy had had no complications and no spotting.

My second miscarriage ended my third pregnancy. My husband and I were trying to have our second child, and this time he was eager to have a baby. I was twelve weeks pregnant this time, and much bigger than I had been the first time, when I miscarried at fourteen weeks. After a full-term pregnancy women tend to show earlier, as the uterus is primed to start growing faster. All my friends and relatives knew about this pregnancy, because it had taken longer than we had expected to achieve. I was still trying to keep it under wraps at work for a while longer. My two-and-a-half year-old daughter was excited that a baby was growing inside Mommy.

Just as before, the miscarriage started with very light spotting. I assumed this miscarriage would be exactly like the last one—over with a bang by the next morning. It was a Monday, and feeling disappointed but resigned, I calmly alerted a couple of friends to be ready to look after my daughter in the next 24 hours, since I figured I would be going to the emergency room as before. Ever the optimist, and always looking for order in the universe, I guessed I had to take two pregnancies for each of my children. My life was just too easy, and I had to pay this extra toll to make up for it. I was surprised when Tuesday came and I had not miscarried. The spotting was still very light. I called my obstetrics office, and a doctor examined me. The good news was that my cervix was intact. The bad news was we could do nothing but wait. The doctor said, "Well, we could do an ultrasound, but no matter what the results are, I won't do anything." I figured there was no point in doing the ultrasound, but in retrospect it might have been a good idea. The obstetrician's advice: "Just relax; many women spot during pregnancy." But I don't. This time the bleeding built up slowly over several days. I kept everyone on alert for four days, each day certain I was going to miscarry.

It was not until Thursday evening that contractions began, and I knew it was finally going to happen. By Friday morning the bleeding was profuse, full of clots, and the contractions were strong enough to warrant light breathing techniques. I was very calm, waiting for the right moment to go to the emergency room. My husband had the day off, and my parents happened to be flying in for the weekend. I did not call them to tell them what was happening. Once again the tough-it-out approach was taking hold of me. I sat in the yard with my daughter, talking to her about the plans for the day. She and Daddy would take me to the emergency room, then go to the airport for Grandma and Grandpa. I needed to go see the doctor because the baby was sick and had stopped growing.

Finally the clots I was passing were getting scary, and it was time to go. My husband and my daughter dropped me off and went on to the airport. When I checked in to the emergency room the nurse insisted that I change from my thick menstrual pad to one of the hospital's thinner ones. Then I had to wait to be examined. Of course by then I was a bloody mess. The obstetrician was new and was wonderfully sweet, although he did not know where any supplies were stored. The emergency room was being remodeled, and I felt like I was in a warehouse. I had a D and E this time, and it was very painful. I used labor breathing techniques, but they were not very effective. It was a difficult several minutes, as I felt my uterus being suctioned out. When it was over, I felt drained but calm. I asked the obstetrician if he had seen a fetus, but he said there were no intact tissues recovered by the suction.

As with my earlier miscarriage, I felt the need to go on with business as usual. It seems I had to punish myself and everyone around me. My husband met my parents at the airport with the news. Over the weekend I insisted we carry on with previous plans, including a boat trip that took two hours each way. That was nauseating, but it would have been if I had been pregnant, too. I was short-tempered with everyone. No one dared to discuss the miscarriage. I ended up making my mother angry at me.

In physical terms the contrast between my first and second miscarriage experiences was dramatic. The actual time course of a miscarriage is quite variable. When bleeding goes on for several days, many doctors will order an ultrasound examination and immediately perform a D and C if there is evidence that the embryo is not alive and the proper size for its age. But even if my second miscarriage had gone as fast as the first, the experience would still have been very different. I knew approximately what to expect. I knew I would miscarry, but I had already given birth to a healthy child. I knew I would have contractions, and I knew their approximate duration and degree of pain. When the bleeding was quite heavy, and contractions much stronger than during my first miscarriage, I was sitting on our patio calmly carrying on a conversation with my daughter. The D and E did not upset me as much, though it hurt much more, because I was aware, experienced, and resigned.

During this pregnancy I was under terrible stress at work. The timing of the pregnancy was not good for the university calendar, and almost every night I had lain awake, anxious at the thought of delivering in the middle of the fall term. There were rumors that some of us lecturers might be losing our jobs after the next year. In addition, I could not feel a connection with the baby. I remembered feeling this connection very early in my pregnancy with my daughter. Though exhausted each night, I could not get to sleep. I lay awake worrying in the dark, asking, "Are you in there?" I was so deep in anxiety that I would fall asleep saying to myself, "Well, maybe I'll have a miscarriage." Well, I did. And the battle between my senses of guilt and relief tore me up.

There are many more complex emotions associated with this second miscarriage than with my first: sadness, relief, guilt, self-defeat. Next came uncertainty: how could I explain this miscarriage, if the first was my "one and only"? I couldn't have actually willed it with my worries, could I? I had to think of a convincing explanation. My doctor wrote it off as "for the best," as usual.

The best I could come up with at the time was that my husband had spent several hours in a hot tub. I had recently read an article suggesting that long hours in hot tubs can cause temporary infertility in men by killing sperm. It was my husband's little joke that he had spent time in a hot tub just before getting me pregnant. I decided the joke was on him when I had a miscarriage. My explanation was not that heat had killed his sperm, because then I could not have gotten pregnant. Rather, the heat caused deficient sperm to be made. This was a nice, neat explanation. I had given myself the blame for the first miscarriage, since I was over thirty-five. Now the score was even. I rationalized that it takes me two pregnancies to make each child. So this had to be my very last miscarriage. Next time we would have a perfect child, just as we had with my second pregnancy.

Even with such rationalizations, having a second miscarriage changed all the rules. Trying to get pregnant lost its magic. Getting excited about a new pregnancy was out. Even though my husband was now happy to have a second child, he said he did not want to make a big deal about the next pregnancy, because I might miscarry. And he was right two more times. There was no point in telling family or friends when I got pregnant each time. They could not figure out how to respond anymore. Of course, there were exceptions. My oldest friend kept tabs on me and was always encouraging me. Even so, when I finally had a normal baby after my fourth try, she said she had privately started to think it was never going to happen for me.

Each time I became pregnant, I could not really believe in the pregnancy. I tried to think positively, but it was difficult. Whenever I walked past a mirror I would look at the person reflected there, and think, "Who are you trying to kid, you fake!" Every time I went to the bathroom I expected to see spotting . I often thought I saw spotting when there was none. After a while checking became an obsession, a habit impossible to break.

The mourning process became shorter after each miscarriage, because I was becoming resigned to failure and did not actually think each pregnancy was real. Somehow, though, I never gave up, but kept on trying. I was very lucky to be able to get pregnant in the first place. Such fertility in a thirty-nine-year-old woman is fortunate. I got pregnant in February, July, October, and December. I could not deny the feeling of hope that came each time I got pregnant. But I would always try to talk myself out of it. It was a constant battle between the two sides of me: the naive little hopeful one and the nasty tricky fake one. After each miscarriage, I went about business as usual. No one else could possibly feel as badly as I did, and besides, I had a sense of terrible shame and failure.

Another problem arises with a miscarriage that comes after having a healthy child: explaining it to your child. My daughter, at two-and-a-half, was very interested in my pregnancy. I had not wanted to tell her I was pregnant so early, but I found myself incredibly fatigued. I could barely get out of bed in the morning. I wanted to sleep all the time. I wanted my daughter to understand why I was acting so lazy and not doing all the usual things with her. How one explains a miscarriage to a child depends on the child's age and degree of involvement. In my case my daughter was very interested, but too young to have a clear concept of time or of death. Nine months meant nothing to her.

I did not think it would serve any purpose to tell her the baby had died, so I told her it had gotten sick and stopped growing for a while. Of course there was a risk that the baby would never grow again, but I decided to worry about that later. And I did have to worry about it, since I continued to have miscarriages. I did not tell her the baby was "growing again" until well into my fourth pregnancy, after two more miscarriages. During that final, successful pregnancy, I always qualified everything I said about our expected baby, until very late, after seven months.

This approach interfered somewhat with my mourning process each time, since I had to go through the next two miscarriages without my daughter even knowing I was pregnant. I felt the burden on her would be too great, if she had to deal with a failed pregnancy each time. Of course she did have to deal with my emotions, though not directly. Whenever I was feeling really sad or hopeless after the later miscarriages, I would tell her I was sad about the one miscarriage she knew about. She had not forgotten it, because she continued to ask periodically why the baby had gotten sick. I told her some babies just do. And she asked when the baby would start growing again. I told her we hoped pretty soon, but we did not know. This need to hear an explanation confirmed again and again is typical for young children. But it got harder and harder for me to recite my little optimistic story to her.

It became increasingly important to me to figure out what went wrong, and what to do about it. This was my personal quest at first, since with my health plan, as in most cases, infertility studies do not get under way until a woman has had at least three miscarriages in a row. I began rather unscientifically to try to figure the angles and to try various changes in my habits. For example, I decided to completely stop drinking alcohol. My previous habit had been not to drink at all in the second half of each cycle, when I might be pregnant. Of course, each time my period started, I would feel the need to let down my perfect behavior. Drinking alcohol was a ritual that went with the beginning of my period, sort of a little wake. Now it became my rule to avoid alcohol all the time, and I tried to convince my husband that he should cut it out too, with some success. My logic was that, at my age, every extra burden on my system reduced the chances of making a good egg, and making enough hormones to sustain a pregnancy. And I figured he should be watching out for his sperm, too.

I stopped lifting any heavy objects, and also stopped all heavy exertion each month after midcycle. This is a very common response to miscarriage, and is indeed recommended in some cases, but it was probably silly for me. I decided I needed to concentrate on my female hormones. For a couple of years I had been keeping my hair short. Now I decided to let it grow out again, to "feminize" myself. Every time I got in the shower I would close my eyes, feel the warm water, and think to myself, "Grow hair, grow. Flow hormones, flow."

Some months I would avoid sex for the rest of my cycle after possible conception, so as not to disturb my uterus. Later I decided to have sex more often after possible conception, as well as more hugging and cuddling with my husband. My strategy was to expose myself to my husband's pheromones. Pheromones are chemicals made by one animal that act as hormones on another animal.* There is probably no reason to take either of these approaches, but by the way, the second approach "worked" for me.

It had not yet occurred to me to read the medical literature on miscarriage, though I had access to it at the university. I was too emotional about my situation to use my science training to tackle my problem. By this time I knew a few other women who had miscarried. One friend's doctor had prescribed progesterone suppositories when she started spotting in her second pregnancy. I thought that might be what I needed. According to my "theory," because of my age I was making just barely enough hormones to sustain a pregnancy. Whenever I became overly stressed, my hormone level would drop to below "barely enough." Thus my uterus would not be able to support the embryo. I wanted to ask my doctor about this the next chance I got.

During this year the anxiety about work continued to in-

---

* Pheromones act on sense organs, such as antennae and noses. It is suspected that humans make pheromones. In one study, a group of women all rubbed a man's sweat onto the skin above their lips, under their noses. Their menstrual cycles, which started out quite varied, all adjusted to the same constant length, the average cycle length for women of 28 days.

crease. I gradually learned that my position, which I had thought was secure, was indeed going to be eliminated. Each of my three miscarriages occurred about a week after some significant bad news about my job. My three pregnancies lasted 12, 8, and 8½ weeks, respectively. I started to feel crazy because I did not seem to have control over anything. I refused to start looking for a new job for the next fall because I was determined to have a new baby by then. It did not seem fair to have to look for a job, when I had been counting on being home with a new baby, receiving maternity leave. Work and my daughter kept me too busy to seek therapy, but I felt a strong need to talk to a therapist about my multiple losses.

During this same year I was in an awkward position with friends who were getting pregnant with their second child. In particular there were three of us who had had our first children at the same hospital within a week of each other. I had been the first to start trying for a second child. One of the two friends started trying much later but got pregnant before me. We were both thrilled when I got pregnant just a month after she did. I called the second friend in this group and joked about getting her husband to let her join our little club. He was not sure they were ready for a second child yet. Of course in May I had to drop out of the club.

Then in October we both became pregnant, probably within minutes of each other, because our cycles were always almost synchronous. This was my third pregnancy of the year. When we met at the pregnancy clinic of our obstetrics group, I was already spotting and expecting to miscarry. By this time the first woman in our trio had a darling six-week-old baby.

Since I had had three miscarriages in a row, I qualified for the infertility work-up at my medical group. Blood samples were taken from me and my husband, for chromosome studies. These came out normal. Next, cervical samples were taken from me to grow in culture. This would test for infections by the bacteria chlamydia and by mycoplasma, a cousin of bacteria. These have been implicated in recurrent miscarriage. As we will see in chapter 11, some obstetricians consider such infections contributing, if not primary, causes of miscarriage. Others, citing medical literature, consider that even testing for such infections "borders on quackery."

The infertility specialist especially wanted me to be tested for mycoplasma. She had herself suffered two fairly late miscarriages, which she attributed to this infection. In my medical group, only positive results are reported to the patient. When I did not hear anything, I assumed all my test cultures had come back negative. I was next to be scheduled to have my uterus injected with dye and X-rayed, an hysterosalpingogram. This is used to reveal anatomical defects of the uterus. But I was pregnant again, so the test was postponed indefinitely.

When I discovered I was pregnant, I was in a panic. I pressed the infertility specialist to consider hormone supplements for me. She told me that there were only very special situations where such treatment would be called for, and that such treatment might carry some risks for the baby. Determined to do something rather than sit by and watch another pregnancy go down the tube, I continued to bother her. She finally ordered an ultrasound examination. She said that if the embryo looked normal in size and development we would not need to worry about hormones, or anything else. At nine weeks I watched the computer screen while my one-inch-long, perfect little baby was being measured, with its big head, and its healthy heart beating merrily away. I stopped worrying about my hormones.

But I did not stop wondering. For the first three months of this fourth pregnancy, I was dropping from fatigue. I had felt the same way during each of the three previous pregnancies that year, each time beginning almost immediately (at 4 weeks, or 2 weeks after conception). I attributed this deathly torpor to my age. I had felt fantastic during my first two pregnancies four years before. Now I could barely get myself going in the morning. All I wanted to do was nap. I took lots of iron, knowing I had a tendency to anemia, but it made no difference. My job stress was finally gone because I had known for certain, since a week before the last miscarriage, that I would definitely not be given a new contract.

I tried to figure out why this pregnancy was an apparent success, at least so far, and if it was related to feeling so awful. I wondered if I felt so bad because I was making plenty of hormones to sustain the pregnancy. Maybe I was more susceptible to the winter viruses that were going around. Perhaps that was good for me, because it made me rest enough to make plenty of hormones and keep the pregnancy going. It was disconcerting to feel so bad, but I was sustained by the healthy appearance of the developing fetus. I never considered the possibility that I might lose a healthy fetus. It seemed that I just had to figure a way to get by with feeling horrible.

At 16 weeks I went in for my prenatal exam. My doctor said he wanted to test me for mycoplasma. He had recently had another patient with recurrent miscarriages. She tested positive for mycoplasma infection, and had given birth to a healthy baby after antibiotic treatment. I assured my doctor that I had already been tested for mycoplasma, but he said there was no record of it in my file. Somehow the omission had gone unnoticed. It turned out that I did have an infection.

I started taking the antibiotic erythromycin at 17 weeks. After five days on the antibiotic, my fatigue vanished. I felt I could carry the world. My doctor insisted there are no symptoms of mycoplasma infection. After two weeks on the antibiotic, I was to discontinue it and be retested for the infection. Five days after stopping erythromycin I felt as horrible as I had before treatment. I called the doctor, and he immediately put me back on the erythromycin. The two-week test results later came back positive, as I expected. Meanwhile, five days after going back on the erythromycin I felt wonderful again.

Erythromycin is not the treatment of choice for mycoplasma. Tetracycline (or the related doxycycline) is much more effective, but it may cause problems of bone and tooth development in the fetus, so is not given to pregnant women. No negative effects of erythromycin have ever been reported. My husband took doxycycline, while I took the much weaker erythromycin. Since these infections are passed back and forth between husband and wife, both must be treated, or the untreated mate will keep reinfecting the other.

At first the erythromycin probably just kept my infection in check, without totally eliminating all the mycoplasma. I took it until 32 weeks, and never felt that awful fatigue again. It is possible that the infection is not reported to have symptoms because women are supposed to feel wretched when they are pregnant. It is also possible that certain strains have more effects than others, or that other contributing factors are involved in creating detectable symptoms of the infection.

About half of all pregnant women test positive for mycoplasma infection. Yet they do not all miscarry. In my case, I suspected it was the added element of stress that gave the infection its force to cause my pregnancies to fail. I will never know if I would have carried my last pregnancy to term without antibiotic treatment. However, I would certainly have continued to have the debilitating fatigue, and it would have taxed me and my family much more, without the treatment.

With a diagnosis and therapy for infection, and a normal report after amniocentesis, I cautiously began to get excited, and let my daughter become excited, too. Slowly we all began to talk about her brother. My husband and I named him. One day, walking by the mirror at about 7 months, I stopped. I slowly smiled at the person there and thought:, "I'm really pregnant, aren't I. No! I am? I am! I'm really pregnant!" Three days before his sister's fourth birthday, my wonderful son was born.

Chapter 5

Trying Again: Getting Pregnant After A Miscarriage

MISCARRIAGE IS A FACT OF LIFE. It is one of womankind's sorrows. Many women who want to have children will suffer miscarriages. With some personal support and confidence that her feelings are valid, a woman can mourn her miscarried child. Through tears and talk, she can begin to heal. Then she must decide whether and when to try again. It is an extremely personal choice, and each woman must go at her own pace, with her own needs in mind. However, in this chapter I will try to convince women who have miscarried to get pregnant again.

In Parts II and III of this book we will learn about the biology of pregnancy and miscarriage, and what medical explanations and help women can expect or demand. But first it is important to consider some practical reasons for pushing ahead with another try. I will relate the stories of some women who have coped with combinations of miscarriage and primary infertility, which is the inability to get pregnant. The stories have different endings, and some are not yet finished. They illustrate some of the hard decisions women must make with little solid information and lots of uncertainty. They show the resilience and perseverance of women trying to have children.

Every woman who miscarries has doubts about her fertility. Very often both husband and wife worry about their ability ever to have children, though it is usually a greater concern to the woman. Such doubts are much less consuming for couples who miscarry after having a healthy child, but they still arise. These doubts deserve serious consideration by women who are over thirty-five, by women who have had several miscarriages, and by women who had trouble getting pregnant in the first place. The older a woman is, the more carefully she should look for clues about her fertility.

If the pregnancy was relatively easy to achieve, taking only a few months, and if it was a first miscarriage, the couple usually focus on getting pregnant again as soon as they feel emotionally ready. When the lost baby is mourned and given its place in their hearts, they try again. Most of the time couples do get pregnant again within several months of the miscarriage. Then their fears center on their current pregnancy. They look for signs that this one will succeed. They begin to get hopeful when the time during pregnancy when the miscarriage had occurred is passed, when they hear the heartbeat, when they see a normal fetus on ultrasound.

There are two groups of women who have a greater-than-average burden of doubt. Unfortunately some individuals fall into both categories: women who have had a long, difficult time getting pregnant, and women who have miscarried before. For these people, it is not at all easy to try for another pregnancy as soon as possible. For women who have taken a year or more to get pregnant, only to miscarry, there is tremendous emotional pain added on to the effort to get pregnant in the first place. For these women, and for those who have had two or more miscarriages, pregnancy itself is somewhat terrifying. Hope and joy constantly battle with a sense of dread. Staying pregnant becomes a frightening challenge.

Any woman who has had a miscarriage, even miscarriage of an unwanted pregnancy, should consider the possibility that it signals potential fertility problems for the future. After a miscarriage, many women are counseled with the pat formula, "You got pregnant once, you can get pregnant again." Most of the time—especially for women under thirty-five, but for most women over thirty-five as well—this is true. But in some instances the miscarriage occurs during a woman's only pregnancy, or her last pregnancy. Of course she cannot know this at the time.

Many women feel that they do not achieve any peace of mind until they are safely pregnant again. They need to prove they are not failures. They need to get past the point of worrying over the new pregnancy by seeing a healthy fetus on ultrasound. So once a woman has healed enough to feel the strength to try again, getting pregnant can complete her therapy. The pregnancy does not erase her sadness over the lost baby. But it gives her a chance to work on the practical problem of having a successful pregnancy. Some women are so wounded by their loss, or by their feelings of inadequacy, that they cannot bring themselves to try again. Their fear is legitimate. But they need to separate their emotions over the baby from their feelings of failure. If they choose not to try again, they deprive themselves of the healing powers of a successful pregnancy. And they lose time that may be running short.

This last possibility is an unfortunate but realistic reason for trying again. The awful fact is that a small number of women will have more miscarriages. They will be caught in the frustrating catch-22 of having to miscarry again before their doctor will try to discover and correct whatever problem is causing the miscarriages. There are few doctors who will investigate the cause of miscarriage after a single one, unless something very obvious was abnormal about the woman while she was pregnant. As we will see in Part III, there are usually no obvious abnormalities, only very subtle ones.

In routine obstetrics practice, it takes a series of at least three miscarriages to start an examination of possible causes. With older patients, usually over thirty-five, some obstetricians are beginning to look into potential causes of miscarriage after two in a row. Very often the next pregnancy is more closely monitored by ultrasound, and if a normal fetus is later miscarried, the obstetrician will begin an investigation. Thus, a woman must try again, as much as she dreads the possibility of another miscarriage. Only if she has one or two more will a detailed work-up begin.

The reality is that most women who do have recurrent miscarriages never get an explanation for them. Yet most of these women eventually have successful pregnancies, without any outside help. When physicians have studied the pregnancy histories of couples with two or three miscarriages in a row, they have also looked at their chances of eventual success. In one study of about 200 couples, 70 percent of those who miscarried at least twice in a row eventually had one or more children. Fifty-five percent, a little more than half, of those who miscarried at least three times eventually had children.

It is difficult to determine the cause of miscarriage, but there are a number of potential causes, and some of these are treatable. Many of the treatments are inexact or even experimental. Most of the time, when a successful pregnancy follows treatment, it cannot be proven that the treatment was actually responsible for the success. Women who have recurrent miscarriages often receive some form of treatment that may not actually be responsible for correcting their problem. In other words, most women's recurrent miscarriages are "self-curing." What this means is that, if a woman wants to have a baby and is going to miscarry once or twice or three times before succeeding, she had better not lose the precious time she needs. This is an unfortunate and tragic reality of life. Somehow, women push on ahead.

In recent years, there have been more and more newspaper and magazine articles featuring women with long series of miscarriages who finally find success after some special treatment. Immune therapy is currently one of the more popular and exotic examples. But what we do not read about in these articles are the much larger numbers of women who finally succeed all on their own. And we also do not read about the women who try these experimental treatments and still cannot carry a pregnancy to term.

My first story is about one woman's ten-year struggle to have children. She had some trouble getting pregnant, four miscarriages, and one threatened miscarriage during the first of two successful pregnancies. She lives in a non-urban area, and none of her doctors ever expressed any interest in determining the causes of her miscarriages, nor in trying to prevent future ones. The reasons for her miscarriages will never be known. Her eventual success could be attributed to luck, willpower, unknown

changes in her physiology, or other unsolved mysteries.
Her first miscarriage occurred at a time in her life when she
was not yet trying to have children. It was 1975. She was not married and was in between birth control methods.

> My periods were very irregular, so I didn't even realize I was
> pregnant, though I was about 10 weeks. I was not in any situation
> to support a baby. One night I began hemorrhaging and passing
> huge blood clots. The cramps were unbearable. I called a friend to
> take me to the hospital. I had a D and C in the emergency room. It
> all happened so fast.

She kept this miscarriage very much to herself, and it was a lonely experience. Her second pregnancy was in 1979, shortly after
she got married. The miscarriage happened at about 12 weeks.

> Although we had not planned for this baby, we had talked very
> seriously about having children, and I had just gotten my IUD
> removed. The miscarriage was physically very much like the first
> one, but this time I knew I was pregnant so I knew what was happening when I began bleeding and cramping. My sister-in-law
> took me to my gynecologist's office. I remember the pain of heavy
> cramping as I waddled in with towels stuffed between my legs.
> The doctor performed a D and C in his office. It was all very cold
> and sterile. The whole process lasted about 45 minutes. It was
> early winter, and I remember how very gray everything looked
> outside when my sister-in-law drove me home.

She was depressed for a few months after this miscarriage. She
and her husband decided to try to get pregnant again. It took them
almost two years. She was pregnant for the third time in 1981.

> At about 14 weeks I started spotting. I refused to believe I was
> losing this baby. We had had such a hard time getting pregnant
> this time that the thought of losing the child was overwhelming. I
> went to bed and lay with my feet up for two days. When my
> bleeding became heavier and cramps started, my husband insisted I go to see a doctor. At this point I wanted nothing to do
> with doctors. The two I had been to in the past gave me absolutely
> no understanding or help with my earlier miscarriages, and only
> left me feeling more confused.

> During this pregnancy I was seeing a midwife who had at-
> tended the birth of a friend's baby. I felt comfortable with her, so I
> called her and told her what was happening. I had hoped for
> some positive words from her, but she coolly advised me to bring
> the "specimen" in for a biopsy when I passed it. "Bring it in a jar",
> she told me. I was in tears and very depressed when my husband
> drove me to the emergency room. Lying there miscarrying for the
> third time I knew something was very wrong with me. Why
> couldn't I carry a baby?

She felt very alone, and wondered what she had done to herself
to cause these miscarriages. She felt her body was rejecting the
babies. She suspected her use of IUDs might be to blame.

> Then after all my losses and mourning I began to feel calloused. I
> felt I couldn't trust anyone anymore. I was both angry and sad
> about the coldness of the medical people. They seemed insensi-
> tive toward me for losing a life. Each time in the emergency room
> it was just another cold quick D and C. "Lie still, keep your mind
> off it, don't watch what comes out." It was eerie and sterile.
> Without the sensitivity of my family, it would have been even
> more devastating.

In 1982 she got pregnant for the fourth time, and carried it to full
term. However she had the terrifying experience of a threatened
miscarriage during this pregnancy. She kept a grip on herself by
sheer determination.

> It was around the third month, and I was delivering some art
> work out of town. My truck got stuck in the snow. After I got it
> out, I pulled over at a rest stop and saw I was spotting. I went
> home and went straight to bed. The thought of losing another
> baby was almost too much for me to bear. I wondered if I could
> possibly go through this again. I refused to call the doctor, because
> he would have said to come in and do an ultrasound.
> I lay with my feet up for a whole week, and just kept thinking
> only positive thoughts: this time it's going to happen, this time it's
> going to happen. Then the bleeding stopped. I went to the doctor
> and had an ultrasound and saw my baby and heard the heartbeat.
> My husband and I were ecstatic. For the next two months I took it
> very easy, and carried my son to full term.

A year later she was pregnant again. It was 1984.

> I was about 20 weeks along and thought I was in the clear. I had no idea anything was wrong. When I woke up that morning I noticed there was some light spotting. I told myself it was like my last pregnancy, and I shouldn't worry about it. My husband and I had heard the heartbeat for the first time at my last appointment. I was scheduled for a doctor's appointment that day. When my doctor checked for the heartbeat he said he was having a hard time locating it. He said not to get worried until I had an ultrasound.
>
> I went to the hospital for the ultrasound. By that time, with all the ultrasounds I had had, I knew what to look for. There was no heartbeat or movement of any kind. I was in a state of shock. They sent me home and told me my body would take over soon, and to go to the emergency room when labor began. By evening the pain had begun. I called my husband at work, and he took me to the hospital.

Since she was 20 weeks pregnant, she was given a hormone (Pitocin) to help stimulate uterine contractions, and then given a D and E.

> When it was over all the memories of my past miscarriages, and my first child's pregnancy came flooding back to me. All of them happened at Christmas time. I went home to my one-year-old and couldn't stop crying. I felt I had been denying it was my fault. I talked with my doctor, my family, my husband. Nothing helped this time.
>
> I am always depressed in the winter anyway, but I was extremely depressed that January. And I was mad at myself for having gotten pregnant this last time. I thought, "I just can't do this anymore. If I go through this again it's going to kill me." We were lucky to have our one child. It was time to get on with my life. This last miscarriage was the worst of them all. I had seen the difference in my body, felt the baby growing, heard its heart beat.

Before that last miscarriage she had thought her troubles were over. After all, she had had one successful pregnancy. She could not think about trying again. But she found herself pregnant again, for the sixth and last time, in 1985.

> It happened so quickly: I miscarried on Christmas and was preg-

nant in February. It was unplanned, a complete surprise. Instead of being worried, I was overjoyed and thankful. But I knew this would be the very last time I would become pregnant. I immediately quit work and did nothing but lie around for five months. I was so afraid of losing this one. But I went full term with no complications. When the baby was 6 months old my husband had a vasectomy. We both knew that we could not survive another disappointment.

Throughout the years that this woman struggled to get pregnant and went through succeeding miscarriages, her doctor said, "It was not meant to be. It is over and done with. Don't dwell on it. Next time it will be healthier." She did sense one difference between her successful and unsuccessful pregnancies, which was that she had very strong nausea with the pregnancies that went to term. Nausea is generally a sign of high levels of hormones, which may be a cause or effect of a healthy pregnancy. No one will ever know the reasons for this woman's miscarriages, or the possibility that her fourth, successful pregnancy might have ended in miscarriage. What is clear is that, with almost uninterrupted effort, it took this determined woman ten years to complete her family.

Some women do not have ten years available when they start trying. If only we all were given crystal balls when we reach sexual maturity. This next story begins with a miscarriage whose tragic significance could not have been known at the time. (Many of the treatments and tests mentioned in this story will be explained in chapters 10 and 11.) This woman was pregnant for the first and last time when she miscarried in 1984. After years of tests and treatments, in 1990 she finally decided it was time to lead a child-free life with her husband.

We decided to quit using birth control after my husband finished graduate school. While we were vacationing in Europe, I got pregnant, I mean right away. It was so amazing to come to the realization that I was pregnant, having all the signs of pregnancy, even during the trip. We came home and did a test, and sure enough, I was really pregnant. Then I went to my gynecologist for her test, and it came out positive, too.

When my doctor examined me she said she wanted to check

some of my cervical cells. She took a sample of some of them. Then she gave me a lecture about, "The mother's health comes first. If you have cancer we have to think of you first." Up to that point, every time I told a doctor that my mother took DES, I was brushed off, told not to worry about it. When I tried to be concerned about it I couldn't get anybody to support my concern. I had a lunch date with a girlfriend in a fancy restaurant, and my hands were shaking so much that I knocked over the tea setting, . Here I thought I was going to tell her that I was pregnant, and all I could think about was this speech from the doctor that I had to think of myself first. I had been so happy about being pregnant. But the biopsy turned out normal, and a few weeks later I had ultrasound and there it was, a normal, healthy little fetus.

Shortly after the good ultrasound news, she began spotting. She went back to the doctor, and ultrasound now showed no life signs in the fetus. The doctor told her to go to bed, even though the fetus had probably died. She stayed in bed for three days and then started to bleed more heavily.

It was Halloween night. My girlfriend came over in a costume, and she was trying to amuse me. She kept talking and talking. I was in a lot of pain, and all of a sudden I realized I was in labor.

She had a D and C later that evening.

I was sort of resigned to what had happened. I was sad, but because I had gotten pregnant so quickly it didn't worry me. After the miscarriage my husband and I felt that there were too many things going on in our lives. We were moving and my husband was starting a new job. So we decided to hold off and use birth control again for a while. Later when we quit using birth control and I didn't get pregnant right away, my doctor said, "You got pregnant once; you'll get pregnant again. Don't worry about it." So I didn't worry about it.

She still could not get pregnant. Her periods were irregular. She tried charting her daily temperature, but could not find a normal pattern showing she was ovulating. Finally her doctor ordered a special X ray of her uterus, a hysterosalpingogram. It took two days of botched efforts and discomfort to infuse her uterus with dye. The hysterogram revealed that she had an anatomically abnormal uterus, probably due to her mother's DES treatments during pregnancy.

> All of a sudden, there on the TV screen was my deformed uterus. They asked me, "Did your mother take something when she was pregnant with you?" I thought, "Have you folks been listening to me?" It was perfectly fascinating to them to see it because it was really exaggerated with "rabbit ears." The doctor immediately started talking about doing reconstructive surgery. I said, "Wait a minute, one step at a time here."
>
> My doctor decided to do some blood tests and measure my hormone levels. Every time I went in for a test, if I was not having my period I would have to get a pregnancy test. Then the nurse would say, "No I'm sorry you're not pregnant," and give me this tragic look. I swore I was never going to have another pregnancy test. And of course every time my period didn't start I could imagine I was pregnant. Every little twinge in my belly convinced me I was pregnant.
>
> It turned out my FSH level was wildly high. The doctor called me at home the week before Christmas and told me I had gone through menopause. He said, "You're not ovulating anymore. I'm sorry. Good-bye," and hung up the phone. Although I went back to him a few more times, he never explained any more to me.

As we will learn in chapter 7, high FSH is not a sign of menopause itself but of impending menopause. There is still a possibility of pregnancy. Over the next year this woman was tested by a reproductive endocrinologist, a specialist in hormones. He treated her for underproduction of thyroid hormone. She still could not get pregnant. A fertility specialist did a complete infertility work-up, including laparoscopy, a surgical technique. Her uterine tubes were obstructed. Finally she and her husband applied to an in vitro fertilization program, and were turned down because it was felt they had too many potential problems. As a final test she was given large, expensive doses of a hormone (Pergonal) to stimulate ovulation. Ultrasound showed it was a failure.

No one will ever know the actual cause of her miscarriage.

Since ultrasound showed she had a normal fetus, it is unlikely that it was a genetic accident. Of the various conditions that this woman was diagnosed as having over the years that followed, it cannot be known which if any she had at the time of her first and only pregnancy. We do know that she was ovulating, and her hormones were normal enough to sustain early pregnancy. The miscarriage occurred late in the first trimester, about 11 weeks.

This is not a story about medical failures but about the un-predictability of each individual's fertility. It is possible that the miscarriage frightened this couple away from thinking about getting pregnant. Perhaps, instead of plunging into grief, they tried to remove themselves from it. They took the miscarriage as a sign that the time was not yet right for children, and they stopped trying for some time. We can never know when and why their window of fertility closed.

They have made their peace with this turn of events, and are going on with their lives.

> We have been going to a RESOLVE support group, and have made a lot of progress. My motivation was not so much to be a mother. I just thought my husband and I could have some great kids together. So I don't feel motivated to adopt. We have decided that we'll make an extra effort to get together with our nieces and nephews, and we'll try not to become too self-centered, try to stay involved in the world and interested in people.

Women and their husbands must look inside themselves to find and deal with their feelings after a miscarriage. They need to learn as much as they can about their physical selves, and con-sider what the future may hold for their plans.

The next story is about a woman who is very determined to have children. She has had three, possibly four miscarriages over the years. Her periods have always been very irregular, varying by up to 10 days in length. She is a DES daughter. Twice in the past she probably had early miscarriages. In both cases she had very severe cramps and lost a lot of blood and tissue. The first time she had not suspected she was pregnant. The second time she was scheduled for an abortion.

Then she married, and her next miscarriage came after she and her husband had been trying to get pregnant for almost two years. Because of her irregular periods she did not realize she was pregnant until she had sudden severe cramps. She went to her doctor, who informed her she was miscarrying. The miscarriage was very early, at about 6 weeks. Her husband was out of town at the time. Since he had been unaware of the pregnancy, he never had a strong reaction to it, but it distressed her greatly. Her next miscarriage was about a year later.

> It was much worse, really traumatic for both of us. I was charting my temperature, and we were making love regularly. It had taken about eight months to get pregnant, and I was 10 weeks along. We had seen the fetus on ultrasound. The pregnancy looked like it was going to be okay. We were both completely attached to the idea of a baby.

She had started spotting at about eight weeks, but knew she had a tendency to spot between periods. She knew there was some chance she might miscarry because of the two or three miscarriages in the past. But the ultrasound performed after she started spotting showed that the fetus was developing normally.

> I didn't totally curtail my activities then, and I don't know why not. No one told me just to go to bed. I did lie down a little, and I drank horrible-tasting herbal teas, and had acupuncture treatments. In the middle of one night I started having cramps. After about six hours I called my doctor, and he said to go to the hospital. I went in and waited on the operating table. I was blown away by the pain. I also had a lot of bleeding. My doctor didn't arrive for a couple of hours. A nurse shoved an IV needle in my arm. It hurt like hell, and I yelled. Then they wouldn't give me any pain killer without my doctor.

When her doctor arrived he performed a D and C, and the pain was over.

Two years after the miscarriage she had not gotten pregnant again yet. For the first year she charted her temperature and used an ovulation test kit, and both showed she was probably ovulating regularly. For the second year she took the fertility drug Clomid, plus progesterone supplements. A postcoital test after six months on Clomid showed that her cervical mucus was hindering sperm, so she began having artificial insemination.

I feel like my whole life the last year has been centered on this. When I get my period, it is an extreme disappointment and I'm mourning. Then three days later I have to start Clomid, which means massive headaches for five days. Then I have a couple days rest, then I have to start the home ovulation test. I also do my BBT chart every day. When the ovulation test turns blue I call the doctor and set up the artificial insemination, which is a hassle, as well as an extra expense. Our insurance doesn't cover it. Then I use progesterone suppositories, which drip all over and burn me.

Then after that I'm in the waiting period, and for me the waiting period is the hardest. I get into hoping. In my last cycle my period came three days later than it ever has. I felt pregnant and thought I even looked pregnant. I started to think I was pregnant. I started bleeding over Thanksgiving, when my brother and his wife were here with their kids. I started my period two hours before we served dinner. Suddenly everything felt black and bleak.

Her doctor thought she might have endometriosis, a condition often blamed for infertility, in which uterine tissue grows outside of its normal location. However, laparoscopic surgery showed no signs of endometriosis. Next, her doctor plans to try one last hormone treatment (Pergonal). If she gets pregnant she will drop everything and go to bed. At the same time she and her husband have spent time researching adoption, and have retained an adoption lawyer.

Even if I get pregnant I'm terrified of losing it. The last miscarriage is all intertwined with my fertility problems. It has become hard for me to separate them emotionally. The last two years have been very difficult, and looking into the future, even if I get pregnant, it's very scary. I feel so emotionally vulnerable. I feel like I need extra care. There's a lot in life you can't control. What I struggle to do is not have the miscarriage and infertility be a black cloud on my life, and take over everything.

One way or another, in the next few years this woman will be a mother. She still has a chance of having a successful pregnancy, although it will be a long and worrisome ordeal. She has started working toward adoption. If she does not become pregnant soon, she will have to make the important decision of when to stop trying. Once again, we have no crystal ball to answer this mystery.

Long-term parenting is a basic part of human biology. Every one of us comes into the world because of two biological parents. Much more importantly, every human who develops fully is nurtured after birth. Each of us witnesses parenting as the first function of our species. Our first experiences are receiving care and communication from our parents. The first people we know are our parents. Children play at being parents beginning at a very early age. The idea of having one's own child begins in childhood.

For this reason the emotional loss of miscarriage is immense, compared to the perceived physical loss of the embryo. It depends on the level of individual attachment—anticipation, hopes, fantasies—of the pregnant woman and her husband. For the same reason, there is a sense of loss when a couple cannot get pregnant. The two weeks of hope based on the possibility of a baby are shattered every time a period starts or a pregnancy test is negative. For a couple with fertility problems, a general mourning goes on over all the cycles of ovulation that do not lead to conception. For the woman who miscarries a pregnancy that took many months or years of constant effort, there is a tremendous loss added to this long-term ache of many monthly losses. It can become too much to bear, and women need to decide when to stop, if success is unlikely.

Not everyone wishes to have children. In today's world, in places where women have some control over their lives, and in the face of overpopulation, it has become acceptable to decide not to become a parent. But in fact that is just what is required of a person: to decide not to become a parent, because it is such a basic part of the human experience. When this decision is thrust upon people who would choose to have children, it is extremely painful.

There is a tough decision-making process for women facing the possibility of infertility. At some point a woman may have to separate her decision about being a parent from her decision to pursue pregnancy. There are a number of traditional and modern alternatives to natural, unassisted childbearing, including adoption. In appendix A, I will discuss the techniques and emotional considerations of in vitro fertilization.

Most women reading this book are recovering from the only failed pregnancy they will ever have. I hope they will take a deep breath and plunge in again. They will soon go on to have a successful one. Other women have had two or more miscarriages. At this point each woman must come to an understanding of her own feelings, her agonies, worries, and doubts. She must think honestly about her hopes for motherhood. When she has read parts II and III, she can look for hints to her potential to have success in a future pregnancy, and find the means to work toward her goal of motherhood.

Part II

Biology of Early Pregnancy

Chapter 6

It Is Normal to Miscarry

Course of events from release of egg to positive pregnancy test.

CLINICAL RECORDS SUGGEST that about one pregnancy in five ends in miscarriage. In fact it is likely that one of every two conceptions ends in miscarriage. What is the difference between conception and pregnancy? Conception is the event that begins pregnancy: it is the joining of egg and sperm, also called fertilization. Technically, a woman is pregnant from the instant of conception. An exception might be the case of in vitro fertilization, where egg and sperm are mixed in a laboratory dish. But at conception neither a woman, nor her doctor, nor her own body knows she is pregnant. When she begins to have symptoms such as tender breasts, fatigue or nausea, and a late menstrual period, she may suspect she is pregnant. But not until she has a positive pregnancy test is she officially, clinically pregnant. The standard pregnancy test measures the presence of a hormone called HCG (human chorionic gonadotropin) in the urine. A more expensive test measures the first appearance of HCG in the bloodstream. In this chapter we will see how conception occurs, and the sequence of events that result in a positive pregnancy test. In the next chapter we will discuss HCG and other hormones involved in pregnancy. Although only about one in five reported pregnancies fails, there are many more embryos lost before a clinical pregnancy test is taken.

A ripe egg pops out of the ovary in a monthly event called ovulation. This happens after the ovary is stimulated by hormones from the pituitary gland. While the egg finishes maturing before ovulation, hormones from the ovary prepare the uterus for pregnancy. They cause the inner lining of the uterus to become thick and spongy, creating a cushy place for an embryo to nestle in. We will learn about the maturation of eggs and preparation of the uterus in chapter 7.

In many mammals,* release of the egg is coordinated with dramatic changes in fluids in the vagina and with special mating behavior patterns. Usually females make themselves available to males, strike certain mating poses, and make a scent that attracts the males. This seasonal or cyclic receptiveness and fertility is called heat, or rut. The more scientific word for it is estrus. *Estrus* is Latin for "frenzy." In humans there are no such obvious signs of fertility at the time of ovulation. Very subtle changes in body temperature can be observed by diligent daily checks. In some women, changes in vaginal mucus are noticed. The mucus is made in the uterus, in the region of the cervix. In a small percentage of women, release of the egg is marked by cramps or light spotting.

The ovary is not connected to the uterus, but it is very close (figure 1). Though the egg is actually released to the outside of the ovary, exposed to the body cavity, it is almost always swept into the uterine tube (also known as fallopian tube or oviduct). This is accomplished by the waving of tentacle-like extensions at the end of the tube hanging over the ovary like fingers around a ball. (Imagine your trunk—shoulders to waist—is the uterus. Put your arms out to the sides, bend them up at the elbow, open your hands and reach out your fingers. Put a softball or small grapefruit in each hand to represent the ovaries.)

If the egg does not enter the uterine tube, it can land in the body cavity somewhere and become a tumor, which is another story. Once in the tube, the egg begins moving slowly toward the

---

* Mammals are animals that have fur on their bodies and make milk for their babies. They include such animals as moles, bats, dogs, bears, sea lions, mice, beavers, horses, zebras, rhinoceroses, pigs, cows, giraffes, whales, monkeys, and humans.

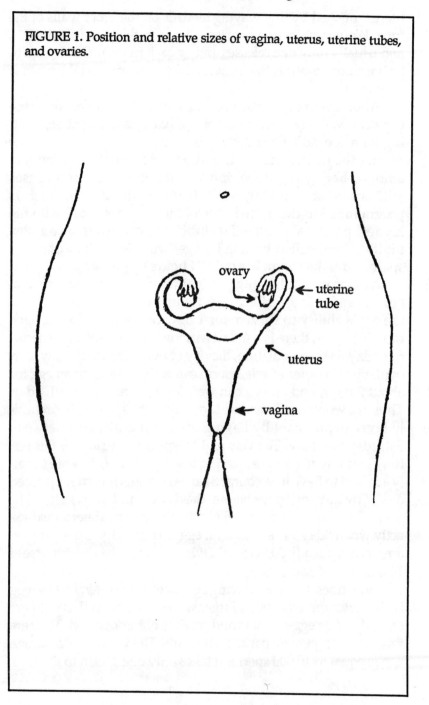

FIGURE 1. Position and relative sizes of vagina, uterus, uterine tubes, and ovaries.

uterus, pushed by tiny waving tendrils on the inner walls of the tube. Women have two ovaries, one on each side of the uterus, and usually only one releases an egg each month. There seem to be hormonal controls that provide for the ovaries to take turns at ovulation.

After leaving the ovary, an egg becomes a miniature Sleeping Beauty, using almost no energy, barely staying alive, waiting for a special kiss. If the egg is joined by a sperm sometime during the next 24 hours, it will become full of life, a human embryo beginning development. If too much time passes without a stimulating visit from a sperm, the egg is programmed to die. Here is one of life's ironies: a cell with the highest potential of all—the ability to give rise to a complex multi-trillion-celled human being—will die for lack of a tiny sperm. And the sperm has only 24 hours to get there.

Numerous studies suggest that human sperm may remain healthy and able to fertilize eggs for up to 2 days. Adding this to the egg's ability to survive for 1 day means that, during each monthly cycle, there is a 4-day window for conception to occur: the 2 days before ovulation, the day of ovulation, and 1 day after ovulation. In other words, sperm can wait around for an egg for about 2 days, and an egg can wait for a sperm for about 1 day. Thus, if a woman will ovulate Monday night, she can theoretically become pregnant by having intercourse anytime between Saturday night and Tuesday night (figure 2). Because of this fertility window, if a couple is trying to get pregnant, they are usually advised to have intercourse 3 times surrounding the supposed day of ovulation: 2 days before, the day of, and 2 days after. The time of ovulation is not at all exact. It cannot be determined exactly when "day 14" starts. If an egg is released at 2 a.m., for example, it is already 20 hours old when a couple has intercourse at 10 p.m. on the same date.

How does the slow-moving egg meet a sperm? While the egg is the potential embryo, a large, well-endowed cell, sperm are specialized as egg-prickers and carriers of information. They are tiny, compact genetic packets with tails. The volume of a human egg is equal to 10,000 sperm. It takes only one sperm to make an

FIGURE 2. Conception scenarios: Each of six women (A through F) has a 28-day cycle and ovulates on day 14. Each woman and her husband make love one time during the week shown (day 10 through 17). Women C and D are the most likely to get pregnant. Women B and E have a very good chance of getting pregnant. Women A and F are very unlikely to get pregnant this cycle.

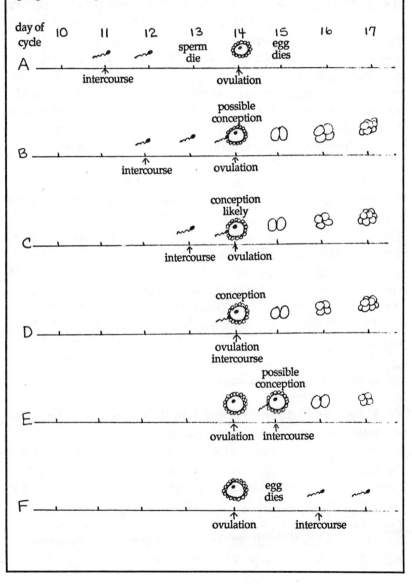

embryo, but to try to make that embryo, a man must ejaculate several hundred million sperm.

Most sperm never get farther than the woman's vagina. Of the millions that do flow through the vagina, most will not make it through the long, narrow channel of the cervix to enter the uterus. The slippery mucus present at the time of ovulation is meant to help them get started. The uterus is a giant sea to these tiny sperm. Sperm have tails with little battery packs that allow them to swim for about half an hour, but most of that energy needs to be saved up for the final approach to the egg. Fluid, muscle action, and the same kinds of tiny tendrils that move the egg in the oviduct push the sperm along toward the top of the uterus (figure 3). A woman may try to assist in this great journey by remaining lying down, or even elevating her pelvis after intercourse.

Finally, a few thousand brave sperm have made it to the top of the uterus. And now half of them will turn the wrong way. Sperm have no way of knowing which uterine tube has an egg inside. About an hour after ejaculation, only a hundred or so sperm arrive in the neighborhood of the big lazy egg, rolling slowly along. Now the band of surviving sperm encounters Sleeping Beauty surrounded by a thick hedge of sticky glue. The sperm surfaces actually recognize and bind to substances in this protective barrier. Then the sperm tips release substances that chemically dig a tunnel through the glue to the egg. Now the sperm use their battery-powered tails to swim through the dissolving hedge. Meanwhile the egg is perched on the fine line between death and life, just waiting for a tiny prick of its surface membrane.

At last, the first sperm through to the egg's surface makes a true union, a complete fusion of two cells, and the mixing of their genetic information into a single individual. The tiny sperm's contribution to the egg's surface is practically nil, but that moment of contact is the signal to the egg to become an embryo by turning on a program of development. The steps of this development into a human baby are dictated by both egg and sperm joined into a single unit: one set of genetic instructions made from two unique and separate human beings.

FIGURE 3. The vagina, uterus, and uterine tubes plus ovaries. The egg is the smallest dot the human eye can see without any aids (smaller than the period typed here). The sperm are much smaller : around 10,000 of them fit into that dot.

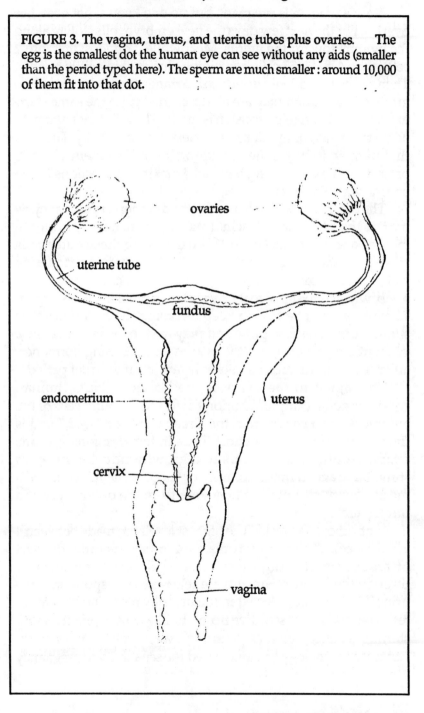

Now a woman is pregnant, but no one knows, not even her ovaries. For the next few days the new embryo rolls slowly along the oviduct toward the uterus. Meanwhile it divides: first into 2 cells, then 4, 8, 16, 32 cells, remaining clustered in a little bundle. Then the cells suddenly decide to rearrange themselves into two groups, and though they are all descended from the same starting cell, another fateful decision is made. The cells that happen to be on the inside of the cluster can develop into a baby. The cells that happen to be on the outside will sacrifice themselves to protecting the developing baby and making connections to the uterine wall (figure 4).

The outer cells will only live for the duration of pregnancy, as part of the placenta, a fascinating organ created by both the mother and the embryo. At this early stage these outer cells release substances to chemically dig their way into the uterine wall, a process called implantation. These cells have an additional job, which is to signal to the ovary that a pregnancy has begun. The ovary must be told to keep releasing the hormones that stimulate the uterus to grow and play host to the growing baby. Without the proper signal, the ovaries stop releasing hormones, and the uterus discards its thicker layers in a menstrual period.

The signal to the ovary is the hormone HCG, human chorionic gonadotropin. Chorionic refers to the outer cells of the embryo. Gonad comes from the Greek word for "seed," and is the site of sex cell production. Thus in females gonad means ovary. Tropin usually refers to a growth-inducing or other stimulating agent. *Tropho* is Greek for "nourishment." Thus HCG means ovary-stimulating hormone from the outer layer of a human embryo. HCG is made from about 9 days after conception until about 14 weeks. The highest levels are made between 4 and 10 weeks. This is approximately 4 to 16 weeks after the start of an average (28-day) menstrual cycle. Hormones travel through the bloodstream and are released for disposal into the urine. HCG can be detected in the urine by a routine laboratory test. The test is most sensitive from 6 to 12 weeks of pregnancy, or starting when a woman's period is 2 weeks late. However, advances in technology have increased the sensitivity of pregnancy

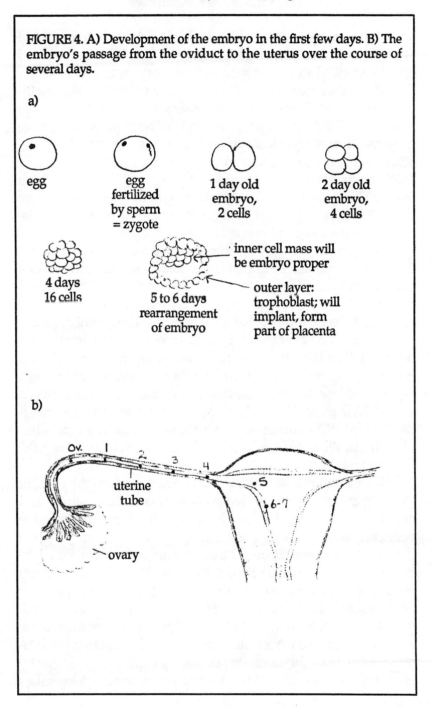

FIGURE 4. A) Development of the embryo in the first few days. B) The embryo's passage from the oviduct to the uterus over the course of several days.

a)

egg

egg
fertilized
by sperm
= zygote

1 day old
embryo,
2 cells

2 day old
embryo,
4 cells

4 days
16 cells

5 to 6 days
rearrangement
of embryo

· inner cell mass will
be embryo proper

outer layer:
trophoblast; will
implant, form
part of placenta

b)

Ov. 1
2
3
4
5
6-7

uterine
tube

ovary

tests. Home pregnancy test kits are fairly reliable when a period is only 1 or 2 days late, and laboratory tests of HCG in the blood can detect HCG almost as soon as the embryo starts to make it.

When a woman has an HCG-positive urine test, she is officially pregnant. Considering that many women who are pregnant enough for a pregnancy test will not have taken one before an early miscarriage, the 20 percent failure rate for reported pregnancies understates the actual occurrence. In one study, early HCG measurements detected 152 pregnancies, 65 of which failed. This is a loss of 43 percent. By standard tests there were only 101 pregnancies, and 14 of these were known to end in miscarriage, for a loss of 14 percent.

Other studies using the same sensitive test for HCG suggest that 25 to 40 percent of implanted embryos are lost before a late period or standard pregnancy test. Thus for every 100 reported pregnancies, 20 of which are lost by miscarriage, there are another 33 to 67 unreported pregnancies whose embryos implanted and then miscarried. Thus 100 reported pregnancies represents 133 to 167 actual pregnancies. Between 33 and 67 were lost before a pregnancy test, and another 20 were lost after a test. The rate of loss of embryos after implantation, then, is between 40 and 52 percent. We might also note that even the most sensitive test for HCG cannot detect a pregnancy that fails before implantation. We cannot determine the number of these "occult" (unseen) miscarriages.

Of all the clinically reported miscarriages, more than half of those that can be recovered and analyzed have abnormal chromosomes. Chromosomal defects are the most likely cause of very early death after fertilization. Such defective embryos have too many or too few chromosomes, rearranged chromosomes, or invisible genetic defects called mutations. Many of these defects are so severe that very early development fails. The embryo may be lost so early that no delay in the menstrual period is experienced. If the embryo lives briefly, the menstrual period may be a few days, a week or even two weeks late. For women who do not want to be pregnant, waiting for these late periods is a nightmare, followed by great relief. For women who want to be pregnant the delay raises false hopes, dashed when menstruation begins.

There are three combinations that can generate an abnormal embryo: abnormal egg + good sperm, good egg + abnormal sperm, and abnormal egg + abnormal sperm. Yet there is only one combination that can generate a healthy embryo: good egg + good sperm. How are defective eggs and sperm made? This will be discussed in more depth in chapter 9. During special divisions to reduce the chromosome number by half, mistakes can be made. Broken chromosomes may be put back together incorrectly. Extra chromosomes may be carried into an egg or sperm, or left out. In chapter 9 we will see examples of these cases of visible genetic abnormalities. These cases are the only well-documented explanations for miscarriage.

We might ask how humans can be so sloppy. We have supposedly evolved to a high level of intelligence and sophistication. It seems stupid to toss out half of our reproductive potential. But by evolutionary standards, what appears as sloppiness is experimentation that can give rise to new capabilities and new life forms, such as humans. There is an incredible variety of mammals, and they seem to have evolved in amazingly short evolutionary time. Apes and humans evolved even faster than other mammals. Apes and humans have almost identical genetic information in their chromosomes. In fact human and ape chromosomes are very similar, except for rearrangements that are products of the kind of experimentation that leads to miscarriage. Humans probably would not be here if it had not been for this natural experimentation.

Most new chromosome combinations are failures. Only a very rare few are useful and contribute to evolution. Most failed experiments result in miscarriage, which occurs in all mammals—deer, elephants, gorillas, and so on—just as it does in humans. Miscarriage of these mistakes erases them. In the unfortunate cases where these experiments do not result in miscarriage, modern humans face the larger problem of caring for severely deformed or mentally deficient children. Still, producing the embryo and growing it to the point of miscarriage means a lost chance for reproduction.

There is an explanation for how humans get away with experimenting with our chromosomes. Mammals are different from most other animals in two ways. First, the male's sperm are delivered to the female during an intimate association we call mating, or sex. Conception occurs protected inside a big strong adult. Second, development of the baby also occurs in this very protective mother's body. Some other animals have the first feature, but few have the second. These two features of reproduction, internal conception and development, greatly increase the chances of producing living children.

Animals with conception and development outside the body have to produce and release thousands, even millions of eggs, as well as sperm, just to give them a chance to get together in the ocean or other body of water. Then most embryos and newly hatched young are completely on their own, at the whim of the weather. They serve as easy pickings for hungry animals.

Not only do human embryos have a better chance of surviving to birth, but we parent our children until adulthood, which also increases their chances of survival. Most other mammals have seasonal mating and reproduction. Babies are conceived and then born when the weather is mild and food is available. They reach maturity by the time the weather becomes harsh. For most animals, it is just a once-a-year chance. Human mating is not confined to a given season. Women ovulate ten to thirteen times a year. Men produce sperm continuously. The loss of an embryo may be tragic to aware parents, but it is absolutely trivial to the species. Very little time is lost—often only two to three months, plus the time of the pregnancy. In fact, some geneticists propose that miscarriage may have had adaptive value in early humans, in helping them space their children so that parental care of the youngest child would be extended.

If we accept the positive side of miscarriage as important in human biology, it raises another question. Why do humans grieve over miscarriage? Is it possible that normal humans do not, that a woman who is deep in mourning for the child that could not be is abnormal after all? The answer is absolutely not. It is important to understand something unique to the human animal: the complete human potential of an individual is not realized without having parents after birth. We humans are the only animals born with essentially embryonic brains. A newborn's brain is anatomically formed, but needs to develop most of its functions through growth of nerves and their connections. It requires experience in the world to finish developing. The most powerful ability of the human brain is to learn. This is a biological characteristic, even a need, not a special privilege. The learning process begins with loving and attentive parents. In turn, being a parent can be a strong human need.

Becoming a parent begins with the idea of a baby. This can be years before a baby is conceived. Children play at being parents. When a woman or man starts wanting a child, she or he has started becoming a parent. When a woman is trying to get pregnant, she imagines her child and when her period starts, she mourns. When a couple has primary infertility—they cannot conceive—the baby they do not make each time they try is mourned, because parenting begins with the idea of a child. So for a couple who want a child, or who began planning and imagining the child in early pregnancy, it is a very natural human trait to mourn the loss.

After having a miscarriage, a woman may feel freakish and alone. Her doctor will tell her it is not uncommon, that one in five pregnancies ends in miscarriage. She may start to find more and more women who have also experienced miscarriage. If she considers the actual failure rate of conceived human embryos described in this chapter, she should realize that it is an everyday part of our normal human biology. As personally tragic as it feels, it is no reason to feel she is a failure, but a healthy member of a fascinating species.

Chapter 7

Hormones: How The Ovaries and Uterus Prepare for Pregnancy

MOST WOMEN TRYING TO GET PREGNANT understand two obvious requirements: ovulation followed by fertilization. The ovary must mature and release an egg, and then the egg must be joined by a sperm. Primary infertility is the inability to achieve one of those two requirements. There is a third necessity for successful pregnancy, and it is not as obvious as ovulation and fertilization. This is the preparation of the uterus for sustaining the early embryo. In this chapter I will describe the events occurring in monthly cycles in the uterus, and their coordination with events in the ovary. Then I will explain the roles that hormones play in controlling these cycles. This discussion will help us understand the importance of hormone actions in establishing and maintaining early pregnancy. It will also reveal some causes of infertility or miscarriage and let us see how hormones can be used to treat them.

Some women do not ovulate regularly; some do not ovulate at all. This primary infertility problem is often due to abnormal levels of one of the hormones required for growth and maturation of eggs. But there are other women who produce eggs and conceive, then miscarry because their uterus is not properly prepared for an embryo to implant. These miscarriages may be occult, occurring so early that the woman does not realize she is pregnant. She may incorrectly assume she has a problem producing eggs when in fact she is having early miscarriages caused by hormonal deficiencies. In chapter 10 we will discuss causes and treatment for a condition of this nature called LPD (luteal phase deficiency).

A. The Uterine Cycle

Most women are familiar with their own menstrual cycles, and women trying to get pregnant are usually aware that ovulation occurs approximately in the middle of the cycle. The timing of ovulation is synchronized with preparation of the uterus to receive an embryo. We can see this more clearly if we remove ovulation and fertilization from the purely natural realm. This is now the routine in a technique called in vitro fertilization, or IVF (see appendix A). Fertilization and the first few cell divisions are carried out in a laboratory culture dish. Then the very new embryo must be introduced into a woman's uterus.

After going to the trouble to harvest mature eggs, fertilize them, and culture the early embryo, it is vital to understand that the embryo will not have a chance to develop unless it is introduced into a uterus that is at the same point in the monthly cycle it would be in a woman who had produced the embryo naturally. For example, introducing the embryo into the uterus during the first 2 weeks of a 28-day cycle would usually not allow survival. The uterus would not be prepared to nurture and receive an embryo. Thus there are two reasons a woman cannot get pregnant early in her menstrual cycle. First, she is not ovulating; and second, her uterus is not ready.

A woman's cycle begins with the first day of menstrual bleeding. The time from the beginning of one cycle to the beginning of the next averages 28 days, which is an old Roman month based on the moon's cycle. *Menstrual* is Latin for "monthly." Nine out of ten women have cycle lengths ranging from 23 to 35 days, but women with cycles as short as 21 days or as long as 40 days can also be fertile. During the first few days of the cycle, the uterus sheds extra tissue layers and blood vessels it has grown in preparation for an embryo. Such disposable uterine linings are made by humans and other primates (chimpanzees, gorillas, and the like). Other mammals build and destroy extra layers in the uterus, too, but reabsorb the extra tissue, so there is no menstruation.

During the monthly cycle the uterus adds about a half-centimeter, one-fifth of an inch, to its walls. This thickening includes soft spongy tissue, blood vessels, and tiny glands that will release sticky substances and nutrients to a new embryo. Other glands in the uterus, close to the cervix, secrete mucus. Around the time of ovulation, the mucus is clear and thin and quite elastic. It can greatly enhance the flow of sperm. Before and after the time around ovulation, the mucus is thick and sticky. This thick mucus is not friendly to sperm, and its main role seems to be to keep bacteria out of the uterus.

The tissue that lines the uterus and is engaged in this growth and specialization is called the endometrium (end-oh-ME-tree-um). *Endo* means "inner," and *metrium* is Greek for "uterus." The first period of thickening of the endometrium, which occurs before ovulation, is called the proliferative phase, because of the dramatic growth of the tissue layer. In addition to its cells increasing in number and mass, the endometrium swells by taking in water and nutritional substances. After ovulation the endometrium continues to develop, but rather than growing much larger, it is specializing. The glands become very active in secreting substances to nourish and protect the embryo. For this reason the latter part of the cycle is called the secretory phase. The wall of the uterus reaches its greatest thickness and fluid congestion, with bloated blood vessels and glands, in the last week of the cycle (figure 1).

A few days before the next menstrual period starts, blood flow to the extra tissue layers of the uterus is suddenly switched off by blood vessels squeezing themselves shut. This causes the tissues they serve to die, because cells cannot survive without being brought oxygen and food energy by the blood. Shortly afterward, blood flow is switched on again, and now the pressure causes the walls at the ends of the blood vessels to burst. The blood and dead tissue fall away and pass out through the vagina over several days. Hormones called prostaglandins cause the uterine muscle to contract, assisting in the shedding of tissue and giving the discomfort of cramps. Within hours of shed-

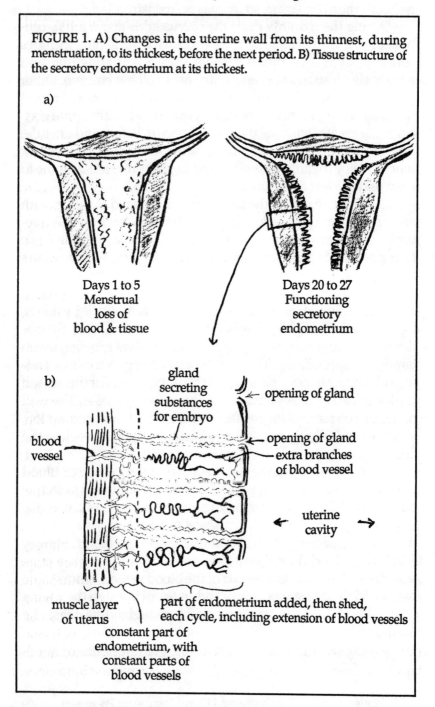

FIGURE 1. A) Changes in the uterine wall from its thinnest, during menstruation, to its thickest, before the next period. B) Tissue structure of the secretory endometrium at its thickest.

a)

Days 1 to 5
Menstrual
loss of
blood & tissue

Days 20 to 27
Functioning
secretory
endometrium

b)

gland
secreting
substances
for embryo

opening of gland

blood
vessel

opening of gland
extra branches
of blood vessel

uterine
cavity

muscle layer
of uterus

constant part of
endometrium, with
constant parts of
blood vessels

part of endometrium added, then shed,
each cycle, including extension of blood vessels

ding its dead lining, each part of the uterus begins building it all over again.

B. The Ovarian Cycle

The ovaries have a cycle of egg growth and release coordinated with the uterine cycle. In each ovary there are many thousands of immature eggs, called oocytes (OH-oh-sites). Girls are born with several million of these, but their number decreases every year. By puberty there are about 300,000 left. These potential eggs can never give rise to more of their kind by dividing. Every day of her life a woman has fewer living eggs than she had the day before. But during her thirty to thirty-five fertile years, at most only about 400 eggs are ovulated, and this is still vastly more than are needed to create an average human family.

Each immature egg in the ovary is completely surrounded by non-egg ovarian cells in a structure called a follicle. *Follicle* is Latin for "small bag" or "shell." At the beginning of the menstrual cycle, several eggs (oocytes) are already fully grown in each ovary. (These eggs actually began growing a month or two earlier.) Each follicle continues to enlarge after the egg completes its growth. From one layer of cells the follicle makes two layers, then more and more, forming a thick sphere of cells around the egg. Then the sphere fills with fluid secreted by the follicle cells. Now the egg sits within the large sphere, on a little peninsula of follicle cells surrounded by fluid (figure 2). The time of follicle growth before ovulation is called the follicular phase in the ovary. The follicular phase in the ovary is coordinated with the proliferative phase in the uterus.

In each monthly cycle, several follicles are seen to enlarge, some becoming almost fully mature. But one by one they stop developing and then degenerate. In fact, many more go through some fraction of their potential growth and then generate. About 1,000 degenerate for every one that completely matures. Most of the time a single follicle continues its growth to the point of ovulation. This one follicle is called the dominant follicle, and it becomes almost solely responsible for producing the hormones

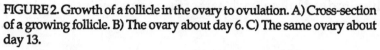

FIGURE 2. Growth of a follicle in the ovary to ovulation. A) Cross-section of a growing follicle. B) The ovary about day 6. C) The same ovary about day 13.

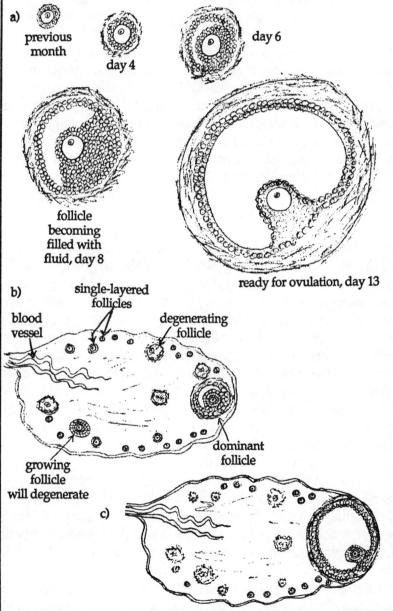

a)

previous month

day 4

day 6

follicle becoming filled with fluid, day 8

ready for ovulation, day 13

b)

single-layered follicles

blood vessel

degenerating follicle

growing follicle will degenerate

dominant follicle

c)

needed to prepare for and maintain early pregnancy.

Although the egg itself is only the size of the tiniest dot visible to the unaided eye, the large spherical follicle is easily seen. It is about 2 centimeters in diameter, almost an inch, an easily visible ball swelling out a good portion of the length of the ovary. Ultrasound visualization of the ovary can determine if and when a follicle is growing and getting ready for ovulation. This technique has become very important in treatments for infertility involving hormone stimulation of ovulation.

In addition to protecting and nourishing the egg, the growing follicle secretes the hormone estrogen. In a normal cycle the single dominant follicle continues to enlarge, literally to a balloon-like state. Then it pushes its way toward the outer edge of the ovary. It bulges out like a blister. The follicle breaks open, along with the edge of the ovary, and spews the egg and small contingent of follicle cells to the outside. Ovulation marks the end of the first part of the ovarian cycle, and occurs about 14 days before the next menstrual period is due. For the majority of women, with cycles between 23 and 35 days, ovulation occurs between day 10 and 21.

An exception to growth of a single dominant follicle occurs when extra hormones are given to a woman to induce ovulation, or to produce eggs for in vitro fertilization. The overdose of hormones causes hyperstimulation, several follicles becoming fully mature. Usually they are harvested by needle and syringe for in vitro fertilization. Such hormone supplements increase the chances of multiple pregnancies. Women receiving high levels of hormones are usually checked frequently by ultrasound. If the ovaries are overstimulated, the follicles form painful cysts, which must be given time to shrink down before hormone treatments begin again.

Most variation in the length of a menstrual cycle is due to variation in the follicular phase. The timing of the cycle after ovulation is much more constant than the timing before ovulation. Most of the time it is 14 days. Thus in most 28-day cycles, ovulation occurs on day 14; in 32-day cycles, on day 18; in 36-day cycles, on day 22, and so on. However, ovulation can occur as late as 12 days, or as early as 17 days, before the next period.

Clinical evidence suggests that the more constant a woman's cycle, the more likely it is that she ovulates regularly, and on the same day of each cycle. If her cycles vary, it is more difficult to plan to get pregnant because the day of ovulation is not the same each month. Some couples want to know exactly when the woman ovulates, or if she does indeed ovulate every month. This is important if there is some reason to suspect a fertility problem, or if she has irregular cycle lengths.

The most inexpensive and noninvasive approach is to use a high-resolution thermometer and keep a BBT chart (figure 3). BBT stands for basal body temperature. The temperature is taken every day at the same time, preferably first thing in the morning, before any activity. During the first half of the menstrual cycle, a woman's BBT is usually lower than 98.6 degrees (Fahrenheit). Then as ovulation approaches, the temperature begins to rise. This may occur over several days, and the higher temperature, around 98.6 degrees, is sustained until the next period, or on into pregnancy. Thermometers that can detect body temperature in fractions of degrees make the changes easier to detect and track.

BBT charts are not quite accurate enough to pinpoint the exact day of ovulation, but they can give evidence that a woman probably does ovulate, and also that the second phase of her cycle, the post-ovulatory phase, is adequate in length. This is signaled by a sustained temperature rise over at least 11 days.

Another home test for ovulation is more expensive but less tedious than taking one's temperature without fail every morning. This is an ovulation test kit. Several different companies now sell these, each kit used for just one cycle. A fairly simple color test of the urine over the course of several days detects the appearance of a hormone called LH. LH is the trigger of ovulation, and its classical surge occurs about a day before ovulation. Most ovulation test kits work best on women whose cycles do not vary by more than three days. Detecting the color change is fairly accurate for predicting the approximate day of ovulation, but again, is not proof of ovulation. It is only a sign that everything seems to be working properly, and ovulation should occur.

FIGURE 3. Example of a BBT chart.

Day Temperature
1   98.0 (menstruation)
2   98.0
3   97.8
4   97.5
5   97.8
6   97.8
7   97.6
8   97.6
9   97.5
10   97.3
11   97.7
12   97.7
13   97.3
14   97.9
15   98.3
16   98.6 (ovulation)
17   98.7
18   98.4
19   98.5
20   98.6
21   98.7
22   98.8
23   98.6
24   98.6
25   98.6
26   98.6
27   98.4
28   98.2
29   98.0 (menstruation)

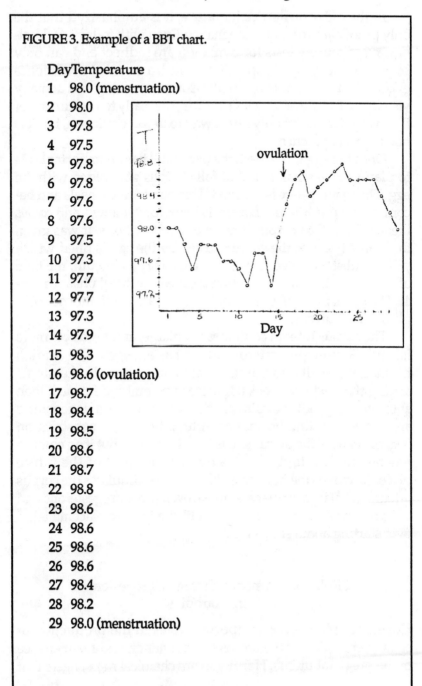

In the older obstetrics literature, it is emphasized that the only proof of ovulation is pregnancy. Even with today's technology, most routine tests for ovulation are indirect and can only show that the system is operating in such a way that ovulation is expected. It is possible to do ultrasound scanning and actually visualize a follicle or follicles rupturing or ready to rupture out of the ovary. This is the only direct way to detect ovulation, but it is not a routine practice.

Once the egg is released, the ovary still has an important role to play. Only a small cloud of follicle cells goes along with the egg. The main sphere is retained. This burst follicle heals and becomes a corpus luteum. *Luteum* is Latin for "yellow," and *corpus* means "body," so corpus luteum is a yellow body. It was given this name because the space vacated by the egg is filled with a yellow substance. Because of the name corpus luteum, the time of ovary function after ovulation is called the luteal phase (figure 4). The luteal phase in the ovary is coordinated with the secretory phase in the uterus.

The corpus luteum continues to enlarge, and produces more hormones, now progesterone as well as estrogen. The ovarian hormones are vital to the survival of an embryo in the uterus during the next few weeks. If there is no embryo formed, then about ten days after ovulation, the corpus luteum degenerates and stops secreting hormones. After a few days menstruation begins again as the uterus sheds its extra layers. But if an embryo has begun development, it's outer layer, part of the future placenta, makes the hormone HCG, which stimulates the corpus luteum to enlarge further and make even more progesterone and estrogen, sustaining pregnancy until the mature placenta takes over starting about seven weeks.

C. Roles of Hormones: Estrogen, Progesterone, Gonadotropins

Hormones play several important roles in the production of eggs, preparation of the uterus for pregnancy, and maintenance of the pregnant uterus. Hormones are chemical messengers that

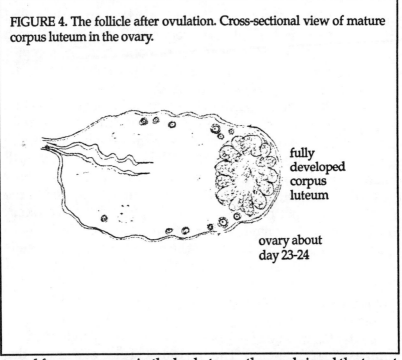

FIGURE 4. The follicle after ovulation. Cross-sectional view of mature corpus luteum in the ovary.

fully
developed
corpus
luteum

ovary about
day 23-24

travel from one organ in the body to another and signal the target organ to perform some task. Hormones are not just used in pregnancy but are necessary for the everyday survival of each person. In addition, the action of hormones makes women different from girls, younger women different from elderly ones, and women different from men.

When a woman takes a pregnancy test, the test is an assay for the hormone HCG. When using an ovulation test kit, the test is an assay for the hormone LH. Women are often treated for infertility or recurrent miscarriages by hormones or synthetic chemicals that have some of the same effects as natural hormones. HCG, HMG (Pergonal), estrogen, clomiphene (Clomid, Serophene), progesterone, and others are used, sometimes in combinations or in sequence, to get around various deficiencies.

Hormones are made by endocrine glands. *Endocrine* means "an internal secretion." When released, the hormones travel through the bloodstream and come in contact with almost all parts of the body. The human body is made of subunits called cells. Hormones contact almost every cell. But only a cell with special receptors for a hormone can respond to it. The receptor detects the presence of hormone and begins a chain of events that stimulate the cell to perform some task.

Each cell is preprogrammed to respond to a hormone in a very specific way. For example, one hormone may tell a certain cell to divide into two cells. Another hormone will tell a cell to produce or release some substance. The same hormone can tell different kinds of cells to do different tasks. It all depends on how the responding cell is prepared. The cell cannot respond to the hormone if it is not prepared to respond, first by having receptors and second by having a response ready. For the body to function normally, hormones must be made in the right amounts and at the right times. Their target cells must be able to respond to the normal level of hormone and must respond correctly. Problems with any of these four aspects can cause failure of an entire process, including reproduction.

Under the middle of our brain there is a tiny gland called the pituitary (pi-TOO-i-tary). Though only the size of a grape, this gland makes more hormones than any other part of the body. Pituitary hormones called gonadotropins stimulate the ovaries. The ovarian hormones estrogen and progesterone stimulate the uterus.

First we will discuss the normal roles that the ovarian hormones, estrogen and progesterone, play in directing the proliferative and secretary phases in the uterus. Next we will see how the pituitary gonadotropins direct the follicular and luteal phases in the ovary. In women these hormones are produced in a cyclic fashion. This discussion will be extremely oversimplified. The variety of tasks these hormones carry out is overwhelming. New ones are constantly being investigated and explained by biologists and physicians.

Estrogen and progesterone are the female sex hormones. They are chemicals called steroids. Steroids are all made from cholesterol, the notorious fat associated with heart disease. Actually cholesterol is a vital part of every animal cell, including human cells. It forms part of every cell's outer covering, the membrane. Cholesterol is also the starting material for making each of several steroid hormones all humans need to survive, as well as the male and female sex hormones. Male sex hormones are called androgens and are related to the steroid testosterone. Both men and women can make male and female sex hormones. A simplified outline of the pathway to make them is as follows: cholesterol can be converted to progesterone; progesterone can be converted to testosterone; testosterone can be converted to estrogen. How much of each hormone an individual makes depends on controlling the steps in that pathway. Men make mostly testosterone and women make mostly estrogen and progesterone.

The steroid sex hormones are ancient. Not only do humans and other mammals use them to be male or female; animals such as frogs, lizards, and birds make the same hormones. There are several different forms of naturally occurring estrogen and progesterone, plus various synthetic forms (those made in chemical laboratories). We will discuss some of these in appendix A.

Estrogen is the hormone responsible for most of the characteristics we associate with being physically female. Estrogen causes girls' breasts, hips, and reproductive organs to grow to adult size at puberty. Estrogen was so named because it can cause mammals whose ovaries have been removed to go into heat, that is, estrus. Thus estrogen generates estrus. Females in estrus are receptive (i.e., interested in) and attractive (i.e., strong smelling) to males. This mating behavior is coordinated with peak ovarian and uterine function to promote pregnancy. Estrus can be seasonal, as in most mammals in the wild, or cyclic, as in most domesticated mammals. In humans it is not clear what effect estrogen has on our actual mating behavior. In fact, the small amount of androgens women make seems to be the main stimulus of sexual desire.

During the time between puberty and menopause, women's ovaries make estrogen in a cyclic fashion, as part of the monthly cycle (figure 5). The smallest amounts are made just before and during menstrual bleeding. Then the estrogen level begins to rise, as the dominant follicle grows immense compared to all the

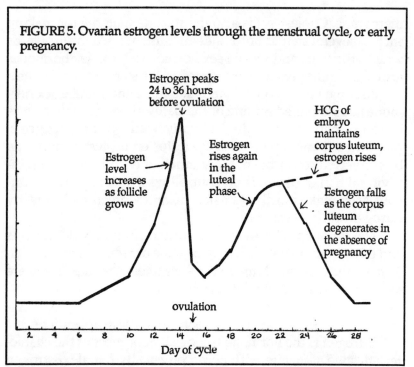

FIGURE 5. Ovarian estrogen levels through the menstrual cycle, or early pregnancy.

other follicles. The dominant follicle makes the major portion of estrogen. During the preovulatory phase, estrogen is the main stimulus for proliferation of the uterine endometrium. Estrogen also stimulates the glands near the cervix to make the clear, sperm-enhancing mucus.

There is a second peak of estrogen production, and this occurs after ovulation. The same follicle, now a corpus luteum, continues to be the source of most of the estrogen. This extra dose of estrogen in the middle of the luteal phase seems to be important for enhancing the secretory phase in the uterus, but also may be required for ending the menstrual cycle in the absence of pregnancy. Estrogen controls production of other hormones involved in the menstrual cycle. This controlling effect is the basis both for using estrogen in birth control pills, and for using chemical estrogen imitators to stimulate ovulation.

Estrogen deficiency is not usually recognized as a cause of miscarriage, but it may be a cause of primary infertility. The role of estrogen is incredibly complex, and many of its effects are indirect. Sometimes when a woman has a fertility problem it only involves a single function of estrogen, and treatment can be based on that single function. There is a difference between having all the electric power go out in a house and having a single light stop working. The same is true of estrogen's many jobs.

In summary, estrogen is most important in beginning preparation of the uterus for pregnancy and for getting pregnant. It is also probably responsible for the breakdown of the corpus luteum and the ending of the monthly cycle in a menstrual period.

Progesterone is most important in continuing preparation of the uterus and maintaining pregnancy. *Pro* is Latin for "in favor of," and *gest* is Latin for "carry," referring to developing a baby. So progesterone means a steroid that promotes gestation. The main function of progesterone is to stimulate the uterine endometrium to continue its specialization into a secretory tissue, so that it can provide for implantation. Progesterone is absolutely necessary for implantation.

Women whose ovaries are removed before 7 weeks of pregnancy will only be prevented from miscarrying by progesterone supplements, not estrogen. There is a crucial time in the menstrual cycle when progesterone levels reach a peak, just a day or two before the corpus luteum begins its rapid degeneration (figure 6). To prevent this degeneration, HCG must begin arriving from a developing embryo. But HCG cannot be made unless the embryo has successfully implanted. So progesterone is required for implantation, and implantation is required for HCG production to keep up the progesterone output, so the implanted state can be maintained.

Unlike estrogen, which has two large peaks of production during the menstrual cycle, progesterone has one small rise, just before ovulation, then a massive rise after ovulation (figure 6). The earlier, smaller dose of progesterone is thought to help stimulate the ballooning of the follicle, along with the weakening of its walls, which leads to the burst of ovulation. After ovulation, progesterone works to change the cervical mucus back to the thick, unfriendly state, to keep bacteria out of the uterus. So

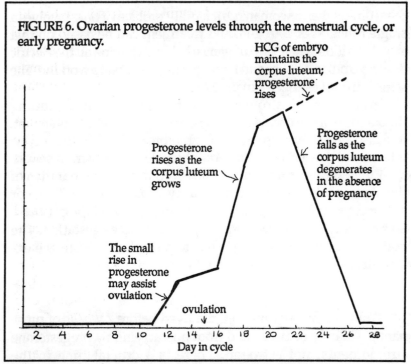

FIGURE 6. Ovarian progesterone levels through the menstrual cycle, or early pregnancy.

HCG of embryo maintains the corpus luteum; progesterone rises

Progesterone rises as the corpus luteum grows

Progesterone falls as the corpus luteum degenerates in the absence of pregnancy

The small rise in progesterone may assist ovulation

ovulation

Day in cycle

the main role of progesterone is to maintain the pregnant state.

While estrogen and progesterone are mainly responsible for stimulating the uterus, the pituitary gonadotropins are responsible for stimulating the ovaries. Unlike progesterone and estrogen, the gonadotropins are substances called proteins, which are chemically very different from steroids. But as hormones they act in a similar way. They flow through the bloodstream, encountering all cells but only acting on target cells that have specific receptors for them. The rise in estrogen levels, the growth of the follicle, ovulation, the development of the corpus luteum, and the rise in progesterone levels are all stimulated, in complex ways, by one or both of two hormones from the pituitary: FSH and LH. These are both gonadotropins, ovary stimulators. FSH stands for follicle-stimulating hormone, and LH stands for luteinizing hormone.

From their names it would seem that FSH works in the follicular phase and LH in the luteal phase. Actually they are secreted during the same period of time but do somewhat different jobs. Although they were named for their effects in women, the identical hormones are made by men's pituitaries and are needed for sperm production. Gonadotropin in men means testis stimulator. In men they are secreted at constant levels. In women they are cyclic.

Both LH and FSH reach peak levels in the day before ovulation. LH is most dramatic in its burst of secretion (figure 7). The LH peak follows the peak of estrogen by a day, and in fact it is estrogen that stimulates this LH surge. Thus estrogen is indirectly responsible for ovulation.

FSH is indeed a stimulator of follicle growth. Both FSH and LH cause an increase in the secretion of estrogen, and LH stimulates the final maturation of the egg and ovulation. FSH assists in the breakdown of the follicle. After ovulation, LH causes the follicle to become a corpus luteum and secrete progesterone. Thus the gonadotropins stimulate follicle growth, ovulation, and secretion of estrogen and progesterone. Estrogen and progesterone then act on the uterus. In a non-conceiving menstrual cycle, the levels of all these hormones fall and menstruation follows.

There is a special part of the brain that controls the pituitary gland, telling it to release or stop releasing various hormones according to the body's needs. This part of the brain is called the hypothalamus. This part of the brain is not used for sophisticated thinking, but controls important parts of our physiology. Here I will refer to it simply as the brain. The brain makes hormones that control the pituitary. So the chain is brain to pituitary to ovary to uterus. In most mammals the main control of the whole chain is at the brain, which is subject to control by sensory input from the environment. This is how fertility and reproduction can be seasonal. In primates the control link between brain and pituitary has become a simpler on/off switch, usually left on. The main controls act on the pituitary, which is not directly subject to input from the environment. Thus reproduction is independent of seasons for the most part.

A linear chain of hormonal command occurs in men, in

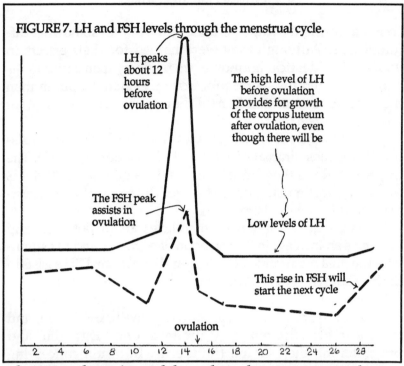

FIGURE 7. LH and FSH levels through the menstrual cycle.

LH peaks about 12 hours before ovulation

The high level of LH before ovulation provides for growth of the corpus luteum after ovulation, even though there will be

The FSH peak assists in ovulation

Low levels of LH

This rise in FSH will start the next cycle

ovulation

whom gonadotropins and the male sex hormones are made constantly by the pituitary and the testes, and sperm are continuously produced. In women there is a loop-back of hormonal control from the ovary to the brain and pituitary. As a result, hormone levels see-saw, and a cycle occurs. In addition to the uterus, ovaries, and other female tissues, estrogen and progesterone also have the brain and pituitary as their targets. The actions of estrogen and progesterone complete the loop of command.

Estrogen stimulates the follicle to respond better than other follicles to the gonadotropin FSH. At the same time, estrogen travels through the bloodstream to the pituitary and causes it to decrease its secretion of FSH. This means that while FSH becomes more scarce, the dominant follicle has an advantage over other follicles, grabbing most of the available FSH for itself. The amount of FSH around would be too small to stimulate growth of any follicle, if every follicle got an equal share. But it is a generous amount of FSH for a single greedy follicle. To the other -

follicles FSH is not really available. These follicles will stop growing and degenerate.

As estrogen increases, the larger amounts stimulate LH secretion. Finally the peak amount of estrogen made by the follicle acts on the brain and pituitary to induce a massive surge of LH. After ovulation, rising levels of progesterone and estrogen act to decrease FSH levels. If there is no pregnancy, the drop in progesterone and estrogen that follows the demise of the corpus luteum causes FSH to rise again and start the cycle over.

If an embryo arrives in the uterus, its outer layer makes HCG, starting about day 23 of a 28-day cycle, or 9 days after ovulation/conception. HCG substitutes for the pituitary gonadotropins and allows a woman to break out of her cycle of menstruation. As figures 5 and 6 show, the corpus luteum in a pregnant woman not only keeps making estrogen and progesterone but increases their levels. The corpus luteum will grow and remain active for about three months, rather than degenerating after less than two weeks. Early pregnancy symptoms result from this increase in hormones: enlarged tender breasts, fatigue, nausea, hunger. The larger amounts of hormones act on tissues that were not programmed to respond to smaller amounts.

Eventually the embryo will stop making HCG. As a result, the corpus luteum degenerates and the ovaries stop making estrogen and progesterone. But these hormones are needed in even larger amounts for the rest of the pregnancy. This function is taken over by the placenta, which starts making them at 6½ to 7 weeks. For about 5 weeks there is an overlap in the functioning of the two glands that provide the needed progesterone and estrogen. By ten weeks the placenta is the main endocrine gland for pregnancy, making large amounts of estrogen and progesterone. The corpus luteum could never generate such large amounts, because of its small size.

As women approach menopause, the number of follicles in their ovaries are dwindling, and the ones that are left seem to be the least responsible to gonadotropin stimulation. In order to produce enough estrogen for ovulation and regular menstrual cycles, the ovaries must have normal follicles and the pituitary must make gonadotropins at the right times. Before menopause, women enter a stage called perimenopause. During peri-menopause, women may still have regular menstrual cycles but not ovulate regularly. If gonadotropins are measured, unusually high levels of FSH are found.

Normally it is high estrogen that suppresses FSH. Under-production of estrogen by unresponsive follicles causes FSH levels to remain high. The higher FSH level is probably not responsible for reduced fertility, but is a sign of reduced fertility. It shows that follicles are not growing properly and that their hormone secretion is subnormal. Often pregnancy is still possible, but fertility is definitely compromised.

When the levels of both LH and FSH become high and remain high, ovarian function has ended. There is no more estrogen and progesterone to regulate the levels of the gonadotropins. Interestingly, the ovaries still make androgens, as do the adrenal glands. Some of this can be converted, outside the ovaries, to estrogen. Individual women make different amounts of this bonus estrogen. Because of this, some women who go through menopause have fewer problems related to estrogen loss than other women.

Women's hormones are produced in tightly controlled chains of command, and in a cyclic fashion that starts at puberty and ends at menopause. Many things can disrupt the chain, causing temporary or chronic infertility or marginal fertility, including miscarriage. For example, some miscarriages are thought to be caused by poor preparation of the uterus or poor maintenance of the uterus in early pregnancy. Treatments to prevent these problems from recurring include synthetic estrogen (clomiphene) and natural progesterone supplements. These treatments are at-tempts to cover numerous possible sources of trouble, all of which have the same end point. It is not always possible to determine the actual source of a hormone problem.

There are complex control paths involved in successful reproduction. Every hormone must be released in just the right amount at just the right time. Organs must respond to normal levels of hormone with the correct response. Each part of the process is a link in a chain of command and interdependence. Biologists are still identifying hormones involved in control of the reproductive cycle. Each hormone's function is not completely defined. While it is unrealistic to expect to have a complete grasp of all the roles of our reproductive hormones without studying them intensely, it is useful to have a general understanding of why an obstetrician prescribes a particular hormone. And it is realistic to know that, because of the complexity of the system, clinical treatment of a woman's problem is often based on general principles rather than a specific understanding of her as an individual.

Part III

*Why Did This Happen?
Explaining and Preventing
Miscarriages*

Chapter 8

Summary of Causes of Miscarriage

Summary of known and suspected causes of single and multiple miscarriage.

WE HUMANS HAVE A COMPELLING DESIRE TO EXPLAIN EVENTS, especially tragedies. People look for order and meaning in their lives, even if it includes assigning blame. Finding an explanation can also relieve a woman of guilt. If she could determine that the miscarriage was not caused by a personal act—long working hours, an overzealous running schedule, or drug taking back in college-days—she could stop torturing herself. On top of this there is a dread of going through another miscarriage, and, even more terrifying, the possibility that she will never be able to give birth. Women seek the cause of their miscarriage so they can take measures to avoid another.

The majority of women will never know the cause of their individual miscarriages. Even a woman who receives treatment may not get an explanation for her miscarriages, and the treatment she receives may not actually affect the outcome of her next pregnancy.

In this chapter I will present a summary of known and possible causes of miscarriage. I will briefly discuss each cause and comment on the range of opinions about its contribution to the miscarriage rate. I will describe them in more detail in chapters 9, 10, and 11, where I will also discuss available treatment. First we need to consider the problem of determining causes of miscarriage in humans. It is also important to understand why obstetricians have difficulty addressing the concerns of individual patients.

The dilemma for obstetricians is that the majority of single miscarriages are genetic accidents, unlikely to be repeated. After one miscarriage, the chances of having a second are the same as the chances of having the first. Of course this rule applies to the general population and not necessarily to an individual. We cannot know the probability that an individual woman will have a second miscarriage unless we know the exact reason for the first miscarriage.

Determining the cause of miscarriage is costly and unreliable. It is not feasible to do this for everyone who miscarries once. After a second miscarriage, the probability of a third becomes greater, because now genetic error is less likely to be the cause than some chronic condition. The exceptions to this rule are women in their late thirties or early forties. Their chances of producing genetic accidents are much higher than younger women. Unfortunately, women in that age group are also more likely to have some other causes of miscarriage than younger women, such as low hormone levels signaling the beginning of menopause. We will discuss the contribution of age to miscarriage more in chapters 9 and 12.

A woman who has had one miscarriage does not know whether this is a one-time loss or the beginning of a tragic series. Based on the average, her obstetrician will tell her not to worry; the chances of a second miscarriage are no greater than a first. But this is not too comforting, since she already knows that such unlikely events can happen to her. Many women long to find the explanation for their miscarriage. They do not want to wait passively to see if they will have another one. They want to know how to act to avoid another one.

While many obstetricians are very sympathetic and will keep a closer eye on the second pregnancy, very few will do any tests after a single miscarriage. Statistically, the expense is not justified. This is a sore point for many women. Such uncertainty adds to self-doubt and dread, and some women hesitate to try again for a long time. Some wait until they feel strong enough to face the risk again. Some secretly hope that whatever bad condition or luck caused the miscarriage will wear off or go away. Some women look for a more openly caring, sensitive obstetrician. Many women try to get some answers for themselves.

A survey of practicing obstetricians reveals that very few possible causes of miscarriage are considered convincing as primary causes by all physicians. One doctor may consider a certain condition to be a primary cause, while another doctor thinks it is only a contributing cause with other factors. A third doctor may consider the same condition not at all important in causing miscarriage. These opinions depend on doctors' experiences with individual patients, the techniques available in their hospital or clinic, their reading of current medical papers, and consultation with colleagues. Conditions that are contributing causes of miscarriage are impossible to pin down scientifically. Such multifactorial explanations are individual, and variable. The discrepancy in doctors' opinions is inevitable, since there are no reliable miscarriage experiments that can be performed on humans and since no complete surveys of human miscarriage have been made.

This is extremely frustrating for a woman who is trying to regain control of her body and her life. With all the new medical technology, how can we not know these answers? Many diagnostic tests are difficult, expensive, and inconclusive. Ultimately the desire to have a baby is greater than the desire to explain the miscarriage. A small number of doctors will offer treatments they consider potentially helpful, mostly harmless, to a woman for her next pregnancy. Most will only treat women with three or more miscarriages.

Very often, physicians prescribe a treatment, such as hormones or antibiotics, for conditions that are possible causes of miscarriage. When prescribing such treatments, doctors may refer to them as "voodoo," "black magic," or "hocus pocus." They shrug their shoulders and make no promises. It is the it-can't-hurt, or who-am-I-to-say, school of therapy. If the next pregnancy is a success, no one will ever really know why.

Many doctors choose not to treat in situations where no diagnosis is possible or if the condition is not a certain cause of miscarriage. Overall, their patients' chances of success are about as good as patients receiving treatment. This is especially true if the cause is multifactorial. Self-cure is quite likely by small shifts of numerous variables. Physical and emotional distress are known to have some influence over our muscle activity, hormone levels, and immune responses, for example.

The following table summarizes some causes of miscarriage. In each category I give an estimate of its contribution to single miscarriages and recurrent miscarriages, whether it is well established or uncertain as a cause, whether it is considered a primary or contributing cause, how the condition arises, when to suspect it, and whether it can be treated.

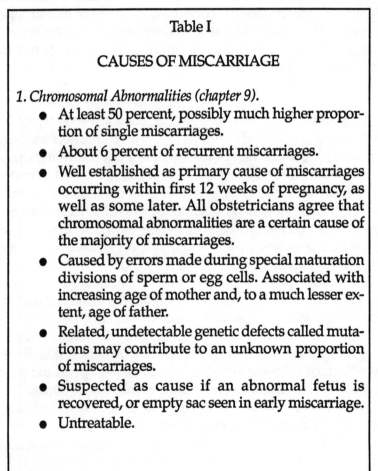

Table I

CAUSES OF MISCARRIAGE

1. Chromosomal Abnormalities (chapter 9).
- At least 50 percent, possibly much higher proportion of single miscarriages.
- About 6 percent of recurrent miscarriages.
- Well established as primary cause of miscarriages occurring within first 12 weeks of pregnancy, as well as some later. All obstetricians agree that chromosomal abnormalities are a certain cause of the majority of miscarriages.
- Caused by errors made during special maturation divisions of sperm or egg cells. Associated with increasing age of mother and, to a much lesser extent, age of father.
- Related, undetectable genetic defects called mutations may contribute to an unknown proportion of miscarriages.
- Suspected as cause if an abnormal fetus is recovered, or empty sac seen in early miscarriage.
- Untreatable.

2. Abnormal Hormone Levels: Luteal Phase Deficiency (LPD) (chapter 10).
- Unknown proportion of single miscarriages, but possibly fairly common.
- Specialists in this field think LPD may cause 33 percent of recurrent miscarriages.
- May be primary or contributing cause of miscarriages that occur before 10 weeks. Fairly widespread agreement among obstetricians that LPD causes miscarriage, but diagnosis in the individual is uncertain.
- The uterine endometrium is not properly specialized to receive an embryo, usually due to insufficient levels of progesterone.
- Other hormone abnormalities may in turn cause LPD. Such conditions are rare but considered real causes of miscarriage, and include underproduction of thyroid hormone and overproduction of prolactin (milk-stimulating hormone).
- Suspected as cause in very early miscarriages, recurrent miscarriages, women with hormone imbalances.
- Treated with hormone supplements: usually progesterone or clomiphene.

3. Abnormal Uterine Anatomy (chapter 11).
- Unknown proportion of single miscarriages.
- Specialists in this field think abnormal anatomy may cause 10 to 20 percent of recurrent miscarriages.
- Disagreement among obstetricians whether each kind of abnormality is contributing cause. Many obstetricians consider that one abnormality, septate uterus, can be a primary cause of early or late miscarriages.
- A variety of anatomical defects can arise during development of the uterus, such as septate uterus, T-shaped uterus, incompetent cervix. Abnormal

anatomy can interfere with implantation or the
ability of the uterus to contain the growing
placenta and fetus, or interfere with circulation of
blood in the endometrium.

- Diagnosed by various imaging or surgical
  techniques for studying uterine anatomy.
  Suspected in women whose mothers took DES
  during pregnancy.
- Surgical treatment is not guaranteed to prevent
  miscarriage, but is highly successful for septate
  uterus and incompetent cervix.

4. *Other Abnormal Conditions of the Uterus (chapter 11).*
- Unknown contribution to single miscarriages.
- Possible contributing causes of 10 percent of
  recurrent miscarriages. Some are more often associated with primary infertility.
- Disagreement among obstetricians whether each
  is an important cause.
- Includes adhesions of scar tissue in uterus
  (Asherman's syndrome), benign fibroid tumors
  (leiomyomas) and endometriosis.
- Most are treated surgically, and obstetricians have
  varying opinions about the effectiveness of surgical treatment for preventing miscarriage.

5. *Infections of Reproductive Tract During Pregnancy (chapter 11).*
- Unknown contribution to single miscarriages.
- May be contributing cause of 10 percent of recurrent miscarriages.
- Many obstetricians do not believe there is any
  solid evidence that infections cause miscarriage.
  Very little is known about the specific strains and
  locations of infection that are most likely to cause
  miscarriage. Many obstetricians think infections
  may contribute to miscarriage with other factors.
- Suspected micro-organisms include listeria,

toxoplasma, mycoplasma, chlamydia, and several viruses. It is not clear whether such infections act by killing the fetus or by causing the mother to go into premature labor.

- Suspected when fever or extreme fatigue occurred during the pregnancy up to miscarriage.
- Some are treatable by antibiotics or drugs before or during pregnancy; some are not treatable.

6. *Immune Disorders (chapter 11).*
- Unknown contribution to single miscarriages.
- Women with lupus anticoagulant (LAC), an autoantibody, have a high rate of second trimester miscarriages. Some obstetricians believe failure to provide a protective immune response to the embryo may cause 40 percent of recurrent miscarriages not explained by any of the causes already listed.
- Women with LAC are treated in the next pregnancy with low doses of aspirin and sometimes with immune-suppressing steroids.
- There is an experimental treatment for women with recurrent early miscarriages who share immunological markers (HLA antigens) with their husbands. Before the next pregnancy the woman is immunized to her husband by several injections of his white blood cells.

7. *Maternal Diseases (chapter 11).*
- Probable causes of single or recurrent miscarriages, though most are rare.
- Diabetes, heart disease, kidney disease.
- Often the mother's health and the developing fetus are carefully monitored throughout the pregnancy.

8. *Environmental Toxins.*
- Unknown degree to which individual or recur-

rent miscarriages are due to toxins.

- Disagreement among obstetricians as to individual causes, since there is very little information available.

- Women working in certain industries are at greatest risk, because of exposure to high levels of various agents. Industries include: metals (copper, lead, arsenic, cadmium); radio & TV (solder fumes); chemical laboratories (various organic solvents); plastics (polyvinylchloride); textiles (carbon disulfide); agriculture (pesticides, herbicides). Other environmental agents suspected of contributing to miscarriage: alcohol, cigarette smoke, rat poison (warfarin), Accutane (isotretinoin).

In the section that follows I will comment on each cause from Table I. I will explain causes 1 through 6 further in chapters 9, 10, and 11.

1) Chromosomal Abnormalities.
As can be seen from reading Table I, there is only one absolutely established cause of early miscarriage, and it accounts for more than half of all miscarriages, perhaps the vast majority of miscarriages. This is the family of genetic defects called chromosomal abnormalities. In studies performed in hospitals around the world over twenty years, geneticists were able to look at the chromosomes of many thousands of miscarried embryos and fetuses.

Summing up all the studies, more than half, up to 60 percent, of the miscarried embryos that could be tested had chromosomal abnormalities. Yet newborn babies rarely have chromosomal abnormalities (about one half of one percent), so these are conditions that do not permit normal development and survival. In fact, the older the miscarried fetus, the less frequently chromosomal defects are found, again showing that these are not compatible with survival. Thus we know that chromosomal abnormalities occur in embryos; we know they are found in large numbers of miscarried embryos; we know they are found in very small numbers in older fetuses and live births.

Chromosomal abnormalities will be described in detail in the next chapter. They are not only the main cause of miscarriage in general but the most likely cause of single miscarriage. Thus women who suffer miscarriage only once before having a child are most likely to have had a chromosomal abnormality as the cause. Table II gives the results of one study, which showed that about half of the single miscarriages that occurred in the first trimester were caused by chromosomal abnormalities. Later miscarriages are less likely to be due to chromosomal defects.

The more miscarriages a woman has without having a normal pregnancy in between, the less likely it is that they are caused by such genetic defects. The exception to this is a very small percentage of the population of normal men and women who carry an abnormal set of chromosomes. These people will constantly be at risk of producing defective sperm or eggs. This is the reason couples with recurrent miscarriages should have their chromosomes analyzed, as we will see in chapter 9.

Table II

Results of one study in which chromosomes
from miscarried tissues were analyzed.

Description of miscarriage	Percent of miscarried tissues with abnormal chromosomes
Before 12 weeks, first miscarriage	*46 percent*
12 to 20 weeks, first miscarriage	*15 percent*
Third or fourth miscarriage	*6 percent*

These results show that the largest percentage of chromosomal abnormalities are found in early, single miscarriages. Women who miscarry repeatedly are less likely to do so because of chromosomal abnormalities.

There is nothing a woman can do to prevent a miscarriage due to a chromosomal abnormality. The occurrence of chromosomal abnormalities is an unavoidable, natural part of our human make-up. Each pregnancy is a toss of the dice, and each of us has the same chances as any other of making abnormal eggs or sperm. There is one unfortunate contributing factor to the bad luck of producing chromosomally abnormal embryos, and this is age, especially age of the mother. Age, too, is a normal part of our heritage, an uncontrollable factor in our pregnancy plans.

Embryos can also have unseen genetic defects, those which cannot be detected by the kind of standard analysis we will discuss in chapter 9. In mice, the best-studied mammals from a genetic standpoint, invisible, single-gene defects have been identified that cause early embryonic death. It is likely that all mammals have similar genes for early embryonic development. Thus, humans can probably have invisible genetic defects that cause abnormal early development, resulting in death.

After chromosomal abnormalities, all other causes of miscarriage become less certain, and each one's relative contribution to the total number of miscarriages is unknown. The reason is that, except for genetic analysis, there is very little scientific evaluation that can be made of large numbers of miscarried embryos, their placentas, or the uteri that held them. Answers depend on studies of the mother, not the embryo, the numbers are smaller, and the studies do not have scientific controls.

2) Hormonal (Endocrine) Abnormalities.

As we saw in chapter 7, at least four different hormones must be doing their jobs properly for a woman to get pregnant and stay pregnant. In addition to causing primary infertility, hormone imbalances are thought to contribute to the incidence of miscarriage. Overproduction (hyper-hormone), underproduction (hypo-hormone) or a poor response to a particular hormone can all cause pregnancy loss.

The main condition in this group is called LPD or LPI, which stands for luteal phase deficiency or luteal phase inadequacy. This condition is difficult to diagnose with certainty. It usually involves underproduction of progesterone after ovulation. The uterine endometrium is not prepared to sustain an embryo. LPD is considered a primary cause of miscarriage in anywhere from one out of four to two out of three women who have recurrent miscarriages. Many obstetricians agree that LPD is an important factor in early miscarriage, especially up to 8 weeks, but is not a cause of late miscarriage.

Women who have some internal or external source of hormonal excess or deficiency are the most likely candidates for LPD. This includes women just beginning, as well as those close to ending, their reproductive years. It includes women taking clomiphene or other hormones to induce ovulation, strenuously training athletes, and women who have recently had a baby, a miscarriage, or an abortion.

From the list of candidates for LPD, it is clear that many women who miscarry because of it may have a temporary problem. LPD is usually treated by progesterone supplements, or clomiphene, and less often by HCG.

3 & 4) Uterine Abnormalities.

For a normal pregnancy, it is obvious that the uterus must be in good condition. It must be able to respond to hormones and to the embryo, and it must be able to undergo massive growth. In addition the uterus must participate in the development of the placenta. If the uterus' physical structure is abnormal, there may be a poor circulation of blood, which will reduce the delivery of hormones. Abnormal uterine structure may result in only limited areas where an embryo can implant.

Uterine abnormalities include malformations such as septate uterus, which is a divided uterus due to incomplete fusion of tubes during the woman's own embryonic development. Another abnormality is T-shaped uterus, which is narrow and constricted, often found in women whose mothers took DES (diethylstilbesterol) to prevent their own miscarriages. Other abnormalities include intrauterine adhesions, which are scars or retained placental tissues, and benign tumors called leiomyomas. There is also a condition called incompetent cervix. An incompetent cervix is not strong enough to remain sealed throughout pregnancy, so the fetus can be expelled very prematurely. Cervical incompetence is only suspected as a cause of miscarriages occurring later than 12 weeks, usually after 16 weeks. Some uterine abnormalities may be corrected by surgery. Most are considered contributing causes of miscarriage, since many women with uterine abnormalities have successful, uneventful pregnancies.

As we will see in chapter 11, some uterine abnormalities are thought to give rise to LPD. The anatomical abnormality does not directly prevent an embryo from implanting or fitting into the uterus. Instead it makes blood circulation in the uterus poor, and progesterone must be delivered by the blood. In this way uterine abnormalities could indirectly cause LPD and give rise to early miscarriage. If a woman knows her mother took DES (diethylstilbesterol) during pregnancy, she may suspect she has an anatomically abnormal uterus.

5) Maternal Infection.
There are a number of bacteria and related infectious agents found in the reproductive tract of women, and men, too. Some of these are implicated in miscarriage, including listeria, toxoplasma, mycoplasma, and chlamydia. Some can be treated with antibiotics.

Researchers studying maternal infections think that miscarriage may be caused by embryonic infection and death, or in some cases by the mother's response to the infection or products of the infectious agents themselves, which result in uterine contractions, causing very premature labor. An otherwise healthy embryo or fetus dies from premature delivery. Maternal infection is most likely a contributing factor with other causes of miscarriage.

6) Disorders of the Immune System.
Two kinds of abnormal immune responses are associated with recurrent miscarriage. One is a known autoimmune condition, the presence of lupus anticoagulant (LAC). The other is a suspected condition, the absence of an immune reaction required to protect the embryo.

Systemic lupus erythematosis, or SLE, is an inflammatory disease characterized by swollen joints, skin rashes, and other disturbances. LAC is found in women with SLE as well as in healthy women. LAC is associated with miscarriages occurring after 13 weeks of pregnancy. LAC may cause miscarriage by damaging blood vessels in the uterine endometrium. Physicians treat LAC with low doses of aspirin, sometimes adding steroids that suppress the immune system.

A new explanation for miscarriage involves an improper immune response to the embryo. This newly discovered cause of miscarriage is controversial, and treatments are experimental.

7) Maternal Disease and Other Causes.
Certain diseases are often considered to cause miscarriage, including diabetes, kidney failure, and heart disease.

Environmental toxins, such as chemicals encountered in the workplace, are implicated in miscarriage but are difficult to pin down. Candidates for causes of miscarriage include: video display terminals (but recent reports suggest they do not contribute to miscarriage), warfarin (rat poison), isotretinoin (Accutane), anesthesia gases, and substances encountered in high levels in various industries, including metallurgy, radio and TV manufacture, chemical laboratories, plastics, textile manufacture, and pesticide production.

Two recent surveys revealed that women who drink alcohol have an increased risk of miscarriage. In one study those who drank at least twice a week had more than twice the miscarriage rate of nondrinkers. In a second study, women who drank one or two drinks a day had twice the rate of second-trimester losses as nondrinkers, and those who took at least three drinks a day had more than three times the rate of second-trimester losses.

Ironically, many doctors deny that stress contributes to miscarriage, but believe that emotional support, represented by extra doctor visits and attention, can result in successful pregnancy after recurrent miscarriages. Recent studies of pregnant women physicians have implicated stress as a factor contributing to the incidence of low-birth-weight babies.

It is important to remember that almost all women who miscarry once do go on to have a successful pregnancy. And the majority of women who miscarry two or three times go on to have a successful pregnancy. Given this information, and the fact that many miscarriages are caused by a bad-luck throw of the genetic dice, most physicians do not become concerned about miscarriage until a patient has recurrent miscarriages. Usually recurrent miscarriage refers to three or more miscarriages in a row. With the increasing age of many prospective parents, some doctors are giving attention to a series of two miscarriages.

The majority of women who miscarry three or more times in a row eventually have a normal child without any treatment. Because of this high "self-cure" rate, about seven out of ten, many doctors are skeptical about any treatment to prevent miscarriage. Historically, it-can't-hurt treatments have sometimes been found to be quite harmful after all. The classic example is DES, given to prevent miscarriage. But each doctor must weigh the suffering caused by each additional miscarriage a woman has, and to keep in mind that three out of ten women with recurrent miscarriages do not eventually succeed without treatment.

Since studies of the nongenetic causes of miscarriage focus on causes of recurrent miscarriages, the findings do not necessarily answer the question of why a woman miscarries a single time. This is also the reason that studies are not very scientific. When a couple has had three or more miscarriages, they do not want to be the control couple in the experiment, the couple who do not receive treatment. Time is passing them by, and if their obstetrician has a possible way to prevent a future miscarriage, it seems cruel to withhold it. This means that studies are usually retrospective—looking back. True experiments must be prospective, working forward with a large number of similar couples, some receiving treatment, some not. In a retrospective study one can never be sure that the treatment itself was responsible for a successful pregnancy.

There are two ways of relating a possible cause of miscarriage to the actual incidence of miscarriage. First, we can look at a group of women who have recurrent miscarriages and compare them to women who have only successful pregnancies. If we find a condition that is common in the miscarriage group but rare in the normal group, it is a possible cause of miscarriage. Second, we can look at a group of women with a particular condition and compare their pregnancy histories to the pregnancy histories of a group of women who do not have that condition. If the women with the condition have a higher rate of miscarriage than normal women, the condition is again implicated as a factor in miscarriage.

In the simplest case, say some condition X causes miscarriage. If only condition X can cause miscarriage, and if X always causes miscarriage, then we should find that women who miscarry all have condition X, while women who do not miscarry do not have X. Similarly, we should find that all women with condition X will miscarry, while no women without condition X will miscarry. Unfortunately there is not just one cause of miscarriage, and there are no absolute causes of miscarriage. We must be careful to understand the difference between a contributing cause and a primary cause.

As a specific example I will describe the outcome of one study into the relationship between miscarriage and abnormal uterine anatomy. We can organize women into two groups: those who have recurrent miscarriages and those who have had only successful pregnancies. When we determine how many women in each group have the abnormal anatomy, the answer is: 40 percent of women with recurrent miscarriages have the abnormal anatomy, but only 5 percent of women with only normal pregnancies have it. This suggests that the abnormal uterus may contribute to the incidence of miscarriage.

Let us look at the same condition another way. We organize women into groups again, but this time the groups are: those who have an abnormal uterus and those who have a normal uterus. Now we ask what the incidence of miscarriage is in these two groups, and the answer is: the frequency of miscarriage in women with normal uterine anatomy is about 20 percent, while the frequency of miscarriage in women with the abnormal uterine anatomy is about 22 percent. There is no significant difference between these numbers. What this means is that an anatomically abnormal uterus is not an absolute cause of miscarriage. An anatomically abnormal uterus can contribute to miscarriage with other factors, or in certain women. But having the abnormality does not mean a woman must miscarry.

Ideally what needs to be done is to study the women with the abnormal uterus who are found in the two different groups: those who have recurrent miscarriages and those who do not. We should find some differences between them that will explain why some women with the abnormal uterine anatomy miscarry while others do not. So far, this information is not available.

There is a third approach to relating a condition to miscarriage, and this is one that uses women with a particular condition and a history of recurrent miscarriages as their own controls. For example, take a woman who has had four miscarriages in a row and is diagnosed with our imaginary condition X. When the woman is treated for condition X, is her next pregnancy a success? We ask this question of all of the women with a particular condition who have recurrent miscarriages, and sum up the number of successful pregnancies out of the total number of pregnancies following treatment. Or more simply the number of live births is compared before and after treatment. A high rate of successful pregnancies following treatment for the condition suggests, but does not prove, that the condition was a contributing factor to the incidence of miscarriage. Though not very scientific, this is as close as most investigations get to being controlled studies.

If the embryo or fetus is recovered after a miscarriage and is abnormal looking, it is very likely to have abnormal chromosomes. In one study, miscarried fetuses with normal chromosomes were examined physically. Almost half of those were malformed and had had arrested development very early. These embryos could very well have unseen, single-gene defects that caused early embryonic death.

We should keep in mind that there is little certainty to date about whether any nongenetic cause can be taken seriously as a sole cause of miscarriage. The most useful source of information in pregnancy today is ultrasound. It has become especially significant in the case of miscarriage because it can tell very early if the embryo itself is developing normally. Essentially, all chromosomally abnormal embryos will show growth retardation at the very least, if not extreme defects or complete failure by 8 weeks, when ultrasound can detect a well-formed embryo with a beating heart.

Many women who have miscarried and have been told it was for the best, that nature was just eliminating a defective embryo, eagerly await ultrasound of their next pregnancy, to see a normal embryo. This eliminates 98 percent of chromosomal abnormalities. If an embryo is normal in appearance, there is only a 2 percent chance that it is chromosomally abnormal. Unfortunately women do miscarry after ultrasound shows a normal fetus. This may be a sign that there is a non-genetic cause. If it is a chronic condition, then it will continue to cause miscarriages of otherwise normal embryos. I hope that physicians will alter their practice of looking for causes of miscarriage only after a series of three or more when they have a patient who loses a pregnancy after ultrasound showed a normal-looking embryo.

Chapter 9

Chromosomal Abnormalities

The most common explanation of single miscarriage.

WE OFTEN HEAR THAT MISCARRIAGE IS NATURE'S WAY of erasing a mistake, and will spare us the misery of having a severely deformed baby who may die in infancy. Defective embryos seem to be quite common in humans for the very reason that they are so easily covered up by miscarriage. Such embryos usually form from defective eggs or sperm, which arise from errors during special cell divisions. The mistakes cause abnormal numbers of chromosomes to be present in the egg or sperm.

In this chapter I will explain how chromosomes are passed from parents to children and how the process can make mistakes. I will describe the most common chromosome anomalies and show how they are generated. Most couples have no reason to expect repeated miscarriages from such errors. Analysis of a couples' chromosomes can reveal the small percentage of couples who can expect to continue forming embryos with genetic abnormalities. For others, only bad luck can cause a second or third miscarriage due to chromosomal defects. There is no way to prevent these mistakes. The only way to reduce their frequency is to be young. Having a clear understanding of this major cause of miscarriage should help a woman feel less at fault and help her accept her loss as an unavoidable misfortune.

All living things are made from preexisting living units

called cells. A single cell divides many times to generate a person containing trillions of cells. Each cell chooses a speciality: to be part of a muscle, a nerve, a kidney, and so on. These choices are made during embryonic development and involve a complex pattern of events. The developmental time course is the same for every member of a species such as humans. We inherit the developmental program from our parents. This is how we inherit characteristics from our parents, because it is through the process of development that these form.

Humans reproduce sexually. Sex has a social connotation to us, but it is also a biological term and means that cells from two parents, two different sexes, unite to form a child. Not all living things reproduce this way. And sexual reproduction is not always social. Trees that are a few miles apart do it. Sea urchins sitting motionless yards away from each other on the ocean floor do it.

The developmental program is dictated by information units called genes. There are many thousands of genes which each of us uses to become human and to function every day. Genes contain not only information for the material parts of cells but also instructions for the proper time and place to construct those parts. Genes are packaged in long chains called chromosomes. The chromosomes are kept in a chamber in the cell called the nucleus. People have 46 chromosomes in every cell except mature eggs and sperm, as we shall see below.

A chromosome can be seen in a standard laboratory microscope. When thickened for cell division, the chromosome looks like a thread. Each chromosome has been duplicated, so it is seen as twin threads. Chromosomes come in different sizes and stain differently with special dyes. Views of chromosomes in the microscope can be photographed. When the picture is enlarged, individual chromosomes can be cut out and arranged on a large sheet of paper. The chromosomes can be matched in pairs and ordered by size and staining patterns. The display of a person's chromosomes is called a karyotype (*karyo* means "kernel" and refers to the nucleus). Two human karyotypes are shown in figure 1.

Humans actually have a double set of genetic instructions. Our 46 chromosomes are two sets of 23. That is, we have just 23

FIGURE 1. A) Karyotype of a male; B) karyotype of a female.

Karyotype of a male

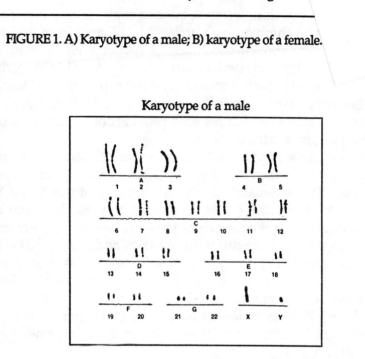

Karyotype of a female

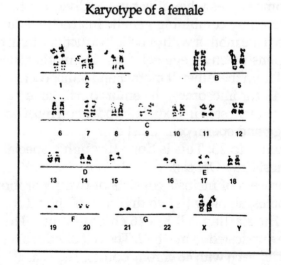

aifferent kinds of chromosomes, but two copies of each one. The information on chromosome number 1 is different from that on number 2, and so on. We need the information on all 23 chromosomes to develop and survive. Our cells only function properly with two copies of each chromosome. (The copies are not identical; they contain the same genes, but may have different forms of each gene.) Mother and father each provide one complete set of 23 chromosomes to the embryo.

As we can see in figure 1, a woman has 23 perfect pairs of chromosomes while a man has 22 perfect pairs and one imperfect pair. This mismatched pair is made up of the X and Y chromosomes. Women have two X chromosomes. The X and Y chromosomes are called sex chromosomes, because they are the chromosomes that are different in males and females. The Y chromosome is very tiny and probably has only two or three genes. These are the male-determining bits of information. The chromosomes are numbered 1-22 (in order of decreasing size), plus X and Y. Thus males actually have 24 different chromosomes. They develop normally though they have only one copy each of the X and Y.

Each cell has a biochemical system for making duplicates of the chromosomes and a mechanical system for separating the chromosome copies when it is time to divide in two. Parents have children by combining genetic instructions (in chromosomes) from the mother with genetic instructions from the father. This happens when an egg cell from the mother fuses with a sperm cell from the father. If mother and father each contribute a cell with 46 chromosomes, the embryo will have 92. To avoid this, an important step in sexual reproduction must occur before sex: the egg and sperm cells must each reduce their number of chromosomes to 23. This is done through a special division called meiosis (my-OH-sis).

The process of meiosis consists of two separations of the chromosomes, along with two divisions of the future sperm or egg cell. The starting cell has 46 chromosomes. The chromosomes are duplicated to make 92. The cell divides once, producing two cells, each with 46 chromosomes. Then each cell divides again, producing two cells each for a total of four cells, each with 23 chromosomes. In men all four cells go on to function as sperm (figure 2). In women one of the four cells keeps the total volume of the original cell while three are little more than fragments, unable to survive (figure 3).

In women the first division of meiosis is stimulated by the pituitary hormone LH and occurs just before ovulation. The second division only occurs if the egg is fertilized. The first division of meiosis separates the matched pairs of chromosomes, so one set of duplicated chromosomes goes to one cell and the other set goes to a second cell. The second division separates the duplicates of each chromosome, so each cell gets one copy of each chromosome in a set (figure 4).

Before the first division of meiosis, all matching chromosome pairs bind to each other. This actually makes pairs of pairs, a total of four copies of each chromosome. In men, the X and Y pair up. The pairing allows for proper separation of the two from each other in the first division of meiosis. A fancy network of fibers attaches to the chromosomes and pulls them in opposite directions. This provides for each egg and sperm to have a complete set of 23 chromosomes.

Each egg contains an X chromosome, and each sperm contains either an X or a Y. Because of the separation of X and Y after pairing, there is an equal chance that any given sperm has an X or a Y (figure 5). The sex of the embryo is determined by the father, with an approximately equal chance of it being male or female. Because of the large size of the X chromosome and the tiny size of sperm, X-bearing sperm must contain about 5 percent more weight in their heads than Y-bearing sperm. It has been observed that Y-bearing sperm are more successful at reaching and fertilizing eggs, but it is not known if the difference is caused by this difference in weight.

If the matching chromosomes did not physically meet at the midline of the cell, there would be no guarantee that a complete set of numbers 1-22 plus X or Y would go to each new call. As an analogy, suppose a person has two sets of an encyclopedia and wants to give one to a library. If the person counts out 26 volumes

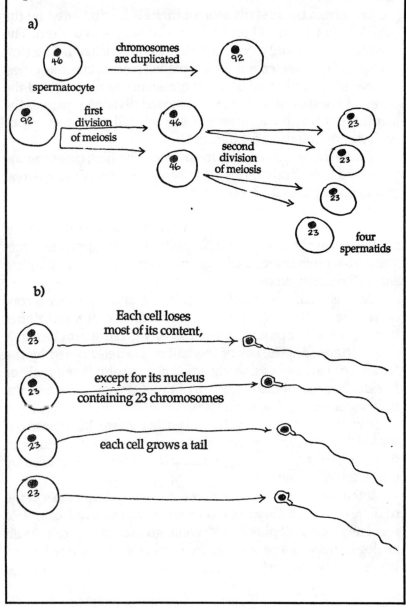

FIGURE 2. Four sperm form from each spermatocyte in men. A) One spermatocyte completes both divisions of meiosis to generate four equal cells (spermatids). B) Each of the four cells specializes into a mature sperm.

a)

chromosomes are duplicated

spermatocyte

first division of meiosis

second division of meiosis

four spermatids

b)

Each cell loses most of its content,

except for its nucleus containing 23 chromosomes

each cell grows a tail

FIGURE 3. One egg forms from one oocyte in women. All oocytes arrange their chromosomes for meiosis before birth. A) An oocyte completes its growth to egg size before meiosis. B) Only one large cell survives the two divisions of meiosis. LH stimulates the first division just before ovulation. C) The sperm's entry stimulates the second division.

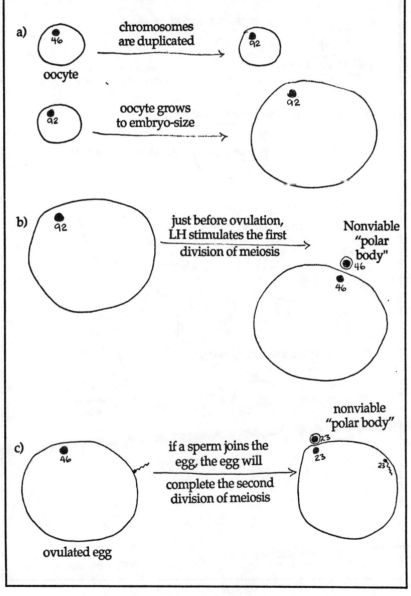

FIGURE 4. Divisions of meiosis shown with just four chromosomes, two each of numbers 1 and 2. A) The cell copies its chromosomes. B) Matching chromosomes pair up. C) The first division separates the pairs. D) The second division separates the copies.

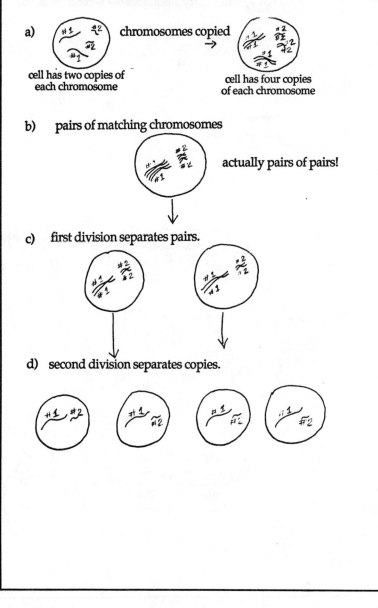

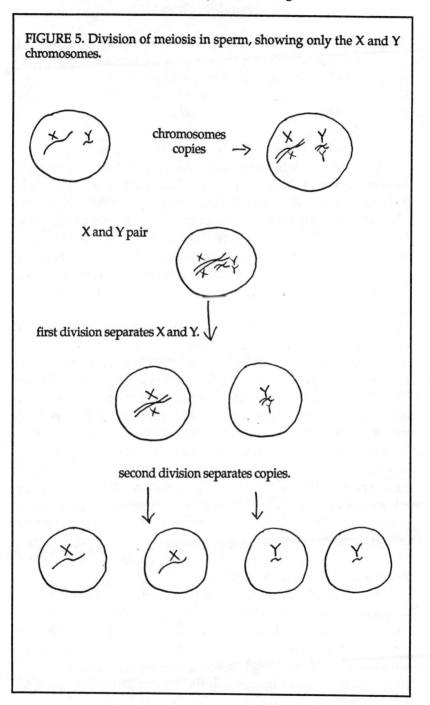

FIGURE 5. Division of meiosis in sperm, showing only the X and Y chromosomes.

chromosomes copies →

X and Y pair

first division separates X and Y.

second division separates copies.

randomly, she might end up with two copies of the J volume, and no copies of the M volume. One way to see that each party gets one copy each of volumes A through Z is to take the two copies of each volume, and deal them out: an A for herself, an A for the library; a B for herself, a B for the library, and so on. This is what the pairing of chromosomes does in meiosis.

Humans have evolved with two copies of each chromosome, and the developmental program is finely regulated to use exactly two copies. If an extra copy of a chromosome is introduced, it is as if one station in an assembly line suddenly increased its speed, while all the others remained constant. The complex interdependent steps of development are thrown out of synch. An even worse breakdown of development results if one chromosome is missing. The more genetic information there is missing or added, the more mixed up development will be, and the sooner the embryo will die. The most extreme case of too much information is one where a whole extra set or two of chromosomes is present in the embryo, so it has 69 or 92 chromosomes.

In most studies of chromosomes in miscarried embryos a few thousand embryos or fetuses have been karyotyped. Overall, half or more have abnormal karyotypes, most of those with too many or too few chromosomes. Most of these embryos are 12 weeks or younger. Fewer chromosomal defects are found in older miscarried fetuses, because such defects usually do not allow survival to later stages of development. There are probably many more very early miscarriages, whose lost embryos are never recovered, that have the most severe chromosome defects. In fact, only about 20 percent of miscarried tissues are in good enough condition for karyotyping. Thus at the extreme, it is possible that the 80 percent in poor condition all have chromosomal abnormalities, for a total of 90 percent.

About half of the miscarriages with abnormal chromosomes have a condition called trisomy (*tri* means "three", *somy* means "bodies"). In trisomy, the embryo's cells have three copies of one of the chromosomes (for example, number 16) instead of the normal two. This gives a total of 47 chromosomes. Trisomy arises from a mistake that can occur in the first or second division of meiosis. It more rarely results from mistakes in cell division in the very young embryo. The error is called nondisjunction, which means the failure to separate. When paired or duplicated chromosomes fail to go apart into separate cells, there will be one cell with two copies of the chromosome and another cell with no copies. When the cell with two copies is fused to a normal egg or sperm, which has one copy of the chromosome, there will be three copies, or trisomy (figure 6).

Trisomy is the most common abnormality found in miscarried embryos. But trisomy can occur for any of the 23 chromosomes. Ignoring the X and Y for a moment, trisomies for all chromosomes except number 1 have been found to occur in miscarried embryos and fetuses. Some trisomies are more common than others. Some trisomies are probably more severe than others and cause death before they reach a recoverable size. Thus there are probably many more trisomic embryos than are counted, increasing the actual number of miscarriages as well as the number that are due to trisomy.

Special staining techniques used by geneticists can sometimes tell the mother's and father's chromosomes apart in the karyotype of an embryo or child. Using such techniques, it has been shown that five out of six trisomies are the result of nondisjunction during egg production in the mother, and only one out of six from nondisjunction during sperm production in the father.

While trisomy usually ends in miscarriage, there is one well-known instance that occasionally allows survival to adulthood. This is trisomy of chromosome 21, one of our smallest chromosomes. The smaller the chromosome, the fewer genes it contains and the fewer functions will be affected. Trisomy 21 is also known as Down syndrome, and most people are familiar with the characteristic look of children and adults with Down syndrome. In addition to mental retardation, Down syndrome children have problems with their hearts and respiratory systems.

Since many people are familiar with this condition, there may be a perception that trisomy 21, though abnormal, is always survivable. But most of the time the extra chromosome causes death during development. This is true of all other conditions of

FIGURE 6. Origin of trisomy and monosomy by nondisjunction, shown for a cell with only 4 chromosomes. a) Nondisjunction can occur in the first division. b) Nondisjunction can occur in the second division.

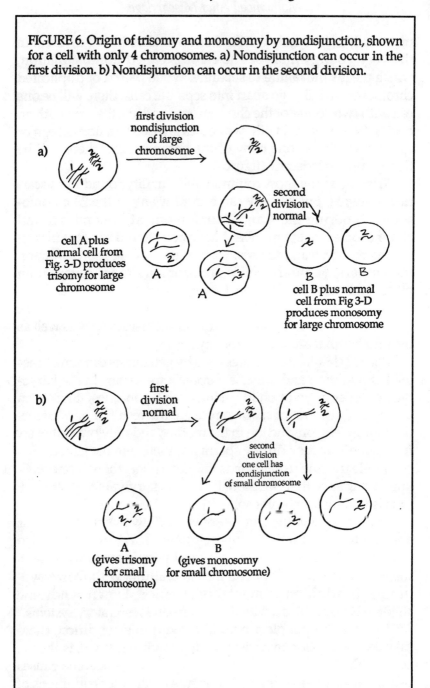

abnormal numbers of chromosomes (except possibly an extra Y). About three out of four embryos conceived with trisomy 21 will be miscarried. Of those Down syndrome babies born, another three out of four die in the first few years of life, most from heart defects. Many Down syndrome children die of leukemia or respiratory diseases by their teens.

Thus out of 100 embryos conceived with trisomy 21, about 75 are miscarried, about 19 die in infancy or childhood, and about 6 survive to adulthood. One in 700 births in the United States is a trisomy 21 baby. This means that about 1 in 175 conceptions is a trisomy 21. There are two other cases of trisomy that, very rarely, survive to birth, but all are severely deformed and die within a few months. These are trisomies for chromosomes 13 and 18. On very rare occasions babies have been born with other trisomies.

Although 1 in 700 births is a trisomy 21 baby, the chance of a twenty-year-old mother having a baby with Downs is only 1 in 2,000. However, the chance of a forty-year-old mother having a baby with Downs is 1 in 100, and it increases to more than 1 in 50 by age forty four. This means the conception of trisomy 21 embryos must be about 1 in 25 for a forty-year-old woman. Other trisomies also occur at dramatically increasing frequencies in older mothers, with the greatest rise in occurrence starting after age thirty five. If the frequency of trisomy conceptions were equal for all 22 chromosomes, women over forty would never be expected to make any normal embryos. By some estimates, the number of embryos with trisomy (not just 21) increases from 2 to 3 percent for women in their twenties, to 15 for the late thirties, then over 25 percent for the early forties. The vast majority of these embryos will be miscarried.

For each egg produced every month by a woman, hundreds of millions of sperm are produced by a man. Men cannot store all the sperm they produce in a lifetime, and they make more by having future sperm cells divide constantly. Women use only about 400 eggs in their reproductive years. We are born with more than we will ever need, and all that we will ever have, several million. Rather than divide, our future eggs continuously die off.

In order to keep dividing, future sperm cells must make

new sets of chromosomes regularly. Eggs' chromosomes are never renewed. They have the original copies made before birth. They can only be rejuvenated by joining with a sperm. It is not known whether women have a special maintenance system for our eggs' chromosomes to keep them healthy over the years. It is likely that we have evolved betting on the chances that, if 400 eggs are used out of several million, a handful should have perfectly good chromosomes, even after many years. For most of our 100,000 or so years of being modern humans, motherhood has come long before the age of thirty-five. Only in the last twenty years has the population of older mothers become large. Our species cannot have evolved a new mechanism to preserve our eggs for those extra years. The extra years of sitting around being exposed to the warmth of the cell plus environmental pollution may damage the chromosomes or the fiber networks used to separate them in meiosis.

Although evidence has not been collected until recently, there is also an association between the age of the father and the frequency of chromosome abnormalities in the embryo. I suggested in chapter 6 that it is part of our evolution to experiment with chromosome combinations by making mistakes in meiosis. Studies show that humans do this even more than other mammals that have been studied in depth; for example, rats. As with many of our body's functions, we lose optimum performance after our reproductive prime in young adulthood. A little chromosome experimentation goes a long way. For forty-year-old parents it often goes too far.

A second look at figure 6 shows us that during a nondisjunction event, there are two kinds of eggs or sperm that are made. One has two copies of a particular chromosome and the other has no copies of that chromosome. There is an equal chance that this second kind of egg or sperm will form and make an embryo as for the first. When such an egg or sperm makes an embryo, a condition called monosomy results (*mono* means "one"). In this case all of the embryo's cells have just one copy of a particular chromosome, for a total of 45.

Since trisomy and monosomy have an equal chance of occurring, we might expect them to be found in equal numbers in miscarried embryos. But monosomic embryos have very rarely been recovered after miscarriage. They must die too early in development. Thus for every 100 clinically detected miscarriages, if about 25 of those are trisomics, there must have been 25 monosomics that died but were not detected. Thus 125 miscarriages probably occur for every 100 that are counted. As we saw in chapter 6, the true occurrence of miscarriage is known to be higher than the clinical figure.

Since all monosomics for chromosomes 1-22 die as young embryos, it is clear that the presence of only one chromosome is incompatible with development. But there is one case in which humans have done quite well with a single copy of a chromosome. This is in the case of males, who have only one X chromosome. The X chromosome is one of our largest and contains thousands of genes, most of which are unrelated to sex. Both males and females must have the information on the X chromosome to survive. But our species has evolved to survive with either one copy of the X, in males, or two copies of the X, in females. Thus we have some way to compensate for the different amounts of information from the X available in each cell. We cannot do this for our other 22 chromosomes.

Because of this difference between the X chromosome and the others, it is not surprising that there is one survivable monosomy: the condition called "XO" or "45,X," where a person has only one of the sex chromosomes, an X. The condition 45, X is called Turner syndrome, and such individuals are females, though they are sterile. They have a characteristic physical appearance that is not as well known as Down syndrome, because it is rarer. Turner women usually have normal intelligence and are reasonably healthy.

The fact that fairly normal people are found with the 45,X condition may again give the perception that there is no serious problem here. But up to one-fourth of all miscarried embryos with chromosome anomalies are 45,X. This is the single most common cause of miscarriage. These embryos are conceived at least one hundred times more often than they survive to birth.

This is a significant contribution to the incidence of miscarriage. One in about 3,000 births in the United States is 45,X, but it is estimated that about one in fifty conceptions is 45,X.

A 45,X embryo can arise the same way as the trisomy 21 shown in figure 6, with X, or X and Y, replacing chromosome 21. The father or mother can generate a sperm or egg missing its sex chromosomes (figure 7). This can occur in either the first or second meiotic division. As we have seen, the incidence of trisomy increases with the age of the mother. This means that nondisjunction must increase with the age of the mother.

Unexpectedly, the incidence of 45,X births does not show this age-related increase. In fact, careful studies that allow us to trace a child's X chromosome to its mother or father have shown that three out of four living Turner girls have their mother's X. Thus the father's X is the missing one. Other studies suggest that surviving 45,X embryos do not lose their X until after sperm and egg have fused. So living Turner embryos are formed by a mistake during their development, changing a normal XX or XY embryo to XO. The causes of this event are not understood, and it may not contribute to miscarriage. But this means that virtually all 45,X embryos formed by nondisjunction during meiosis are miscarried. And this is a fairly common event, as we just saw.

Nondisjunction of sex chromosomes can also generate YO, 45,Y embryos. These are never seen, and probably die even earlier than other monosomics, since they do not have even one copy of the X, which is vital to survival. There are also sex chromosome trisomies: 47,XXY, 47,XYY, and 47,XXX. A second look at figure 7 shows the kinds of nondisjunction that can produce XX, XY and YY sperm, or XX eggs. XYY (male) and XXX (female) individuals range from completely normal to slightly reduced in intelligence with some infertility. XXY are sterile males with some feminized features (Klinefelter syndrome). These are not often seen in miscarried embryos, and their contribution to the incidence of miscarriage appears to be slight compared to 45, X.

About one out of five miscarried embryos with abnormal chromosomes have a condition called polyploidy (*poly* means

FIGURE 7. Origin of XO embryos by nondisjunction. This also shows the origin of XXY, XXX and XYY embryos.

A. nondisjunction of egg's X chromosomes. Each of the four products of meiosis has an equal chance of being in the surviving egg.

	nondisjunction of Egg's X pair in first division				nondisjunction of Egg's X copies (one) in second div.			
Egg	XX	XX	O	O	XX	O	X	X
Sperm	X	Y	X	Y	(X or Y)	X	Y	
Embryo	XXX	XXY	**XO**	YO	XXX or XXY	**XO** or YO	XX	XY

B. nondisjunction of sperm's X-Y pair in first division.

	nondisjunction of X-Y pair in first division			
Egg	X	X	X	X
Sperm	XY	XY	O	O
Embryo	XXY	XXY	**XO**	**XO**

C. nondisjunction of sperm's X or Y copies in second division.

	nondisjunction of X copies in second div.				nondisjunction of Y copies in second div.			
Egg	X	X	X	X	X	X	X	X
Sperm	XX	O	Y	Y	X	X	YY	O
Embryo	XXX	**XO**	XY	XY	XX	XX	XYY	**XO**

"many," *ploidy* refers to a set of chromosomes). These are embryos that have more than two sets of chromosomes. Triploids, which are the more common, have three copies of each chromosome, for a total of 69.

About one in five triploids is generated by eggs or sperm containing two complete sets of chromosomes, the result of nondisjunction of all chromosomes in the first or second division of meiosis. But most of the time such embryos do not arise from mistakes in meiosis. Four out of five triploids result from fertilization of one egg by two sperm. The union of one sperm with an egg is generally able to trigger a change in the egg so that no more sperm can enter. However, it is possible for two sperm to make contact with an egg at the same instant. This yields an embryo with three copies of each chromosome.

Tetraploids have four copies of each chromosome, for a total of 92. Tetraploids are made by complete nondisjunction during division of the early embryo, which started out with the normal two sets of chromosomes. Neither triploidy nor tetraploidy is a survivable condition. Only very rarely do such fetuses develop to birth, only to die immediately from severe deformities.

If a couple has had a clinically detected miscarriage, there is at least a 50-percent chance that it is due to chromosome anomalies in the embryo. If the couple is in their twenties, the chance is really about 35 percent, and if they are in their late thirties or early forties, the chance is at least 60 percent.

There is one group of people who have a very high risk of repeated miscarriage due to chromosome anomalies. This is only about 6 percent of couples who experience repeated miscarriages, (which is about one percent of couples who miscarry), so it is quite rare. These are normal people who have unusual chromosome structures, which came about by breakages of a chromosome in the egg or sperm that formed them.

When chromosomes break, the cell can repair them. That is a handy function, but sometimes the chromosome pieces have moved around a bit before they are put back together, and they are joined in the wrong place. A segment may be pasted onto another chromosome, or pasted onto its own chromosome but

turned around end-for-end. These mistakes are called translocations and inversions (figure 8). Chromosomes break when cells
are exposed to X rays, radioactive substances, cancer-causing
chemicals, and other unknown pollutants. When cells sit around
for many years, as women's future eggs do, the chromosomes
have more exposure to such agents.

Often when chromosomes are rearranged, the embryo that is
made will be abnormal and die, causing a miscarriage. Two to
three out of a hundred miscarried embryos with abnormal
chromosomes have such "unbalanced" rearrangements. This is
usually a one-time bad luck occurrence, just as are the defects we
discussed earlier.

Sometimes the break in the chromosome is at a place where
no harm is done, and a perfectly normal person results. This person has a balanced rearrangement. A person with a balanced
rearrangement has an unusual chromosome composition. One
set of chromosomes has no rearrangements. That set came from
the parent whose egg or sperm had no broken chromosomes.
Another set has the rearranged chromosome or chromosomes.
The two sets must pair up for meiosis. Chromosomes are very
faithful at pairing up all matching parts, even if this involves
forming loops or pairing parts of three or four chromosomes.

Since paired chromosomes often exchange parts, some very
strange chromosomes can result when they are separated. When
a straight chromosome and a looped chromosome exchange
parts, the result will be egg or sperm cells that have some extra or
missing segments of chromosomes. Segments of chromosomes
may contain hundreds of genes, depending on their size, so there
will be the same problems we saw for trisomy or monosomy.
Every time one of these eggs or sperm is used to make an
embryo, a miscarriage is likely to occur. If one member of a
couple has the rearranged chromosomes, there is a high chance
of producing such faulty eggs or sperm—about 50 percent.

When couples have a series of miscarriages, careful study of
their chromosomes is advised to see if one of them has rearranged chromosomes. Although this is rare, the small number
of people who do have this condition can be counseled. They

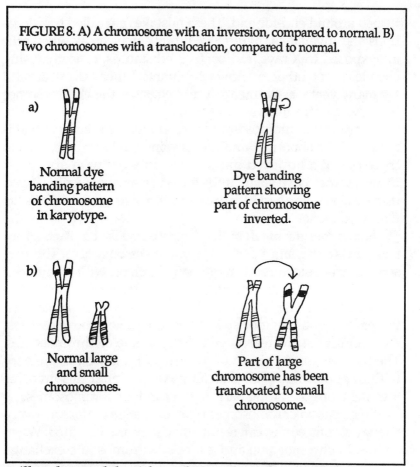

FIGURE 8. A) A chromosome with an inversion, compared to normal. B) Two chromosomes with a translocation, compared to normal.

a)

Normal dye banding pattern of chromosome in karyotype.

Dye banding pattern showing part of chromosome inverted.

b)

Normal large and small chromosomes.

Part of large chromosome has been translocated to small chromosome.

will understand the risks each time they try to have a baby.

Chromosome anomalies described in this chapter are the only absolutely documented causes of miscarriage. Most women who miscarry will not learn whether their lost embryo has abnormal chromosomes or not. If the embryo or fetus is recovered intact and found to be very abnormal in form, that strongly suggests that it has chromosomal anomalies. Ultrasound performed during pregnancy can also give information about the embryo's possible genetic state. If it is a normal embryo, there is a very small chance it has a chromosomal defect. It there is an empty sac, or a deformed or smaller-than-normal embryo, there is a good chance it has chromosomal abnormalities.

Unless there are clear signs of a particular medical problem, when a woman has a single miscarriage, her obstetrician will assume it was caused by a chromosomal mistake. The chances of this being the cause are especially high if a woman and her mate are over 35. There is no way to prevent miscarriage caused by these chromosomal mistakes. They are truly the result of bad luck. The most a woman can do is understand that this is common, and part of our human inheritance. It is not anyone's fault. There is no available treatment or prevention.

The more in tune with her body a woman is, and the more eager to be pregnant, the more often she will detect an early miscarriage, which is most likely to be caused by chromosome anomalies. She should mourn her loss, and know that the next roll of her dice will probably bring better luck.

Chapter 10

Luteal Phase Deficiency, A Nongenetic Cause of Miscarriage

WOMEN WHO MISCARRY A SINGLE TIME ARE TOLD that the most likely cause was a chromosomal abnormality. Depending on their age, they may not need to worry that they will have another miscarriage. Women who miscarry several times are considered more likely to have a nongenetic basis for their miscarriages. In contrast to the certainty that chromosomal abnormalities cause miscarriage, there is much uncertainty about all nongenetic causes.

One nongenetic condition is very often considered as a possible cause of miscarriage. This condition is called LPD or LPI, which stands for luteal phase deficiency or luteal phase inadequacy. In this chapter I will describe how luteal phase deficiency is characterized in current medical literature and understood by practicing obstetricians. I will explain how the condition can arise and how it affects pregnancy. I will describe how it is diagnosed, and when and how it is treated.

I have given luteal phase deficiency its own chapter even though there is disagreement among obstetricians about its contribution to the incidence of miscarriage. LPD is difficult to diagnose, but theoretically easy to treat. When there is an easy treatment available, rigorous diagnosis may be omitted. From reading of the medical literature and discussions with obstetricians and reproductive endocrinologists, I believe that LPD is a real condition and a cause of miscarriage. From my perspective as a biologist, LPD seems to be a natural part of human biology and, if it could be carefully studied, I believe its incidence would be found to increase with a woman's age. Thus it may be quite normal to miscarry occasionally because of LPD, just as we know it is normal to miscarry occasionally because of chromosomal abnormalities.

There are known to be two classes of couples who have miscarriages caused by chromosomal abnormalities. For the majority of couples it is an isolated, random event. A small percentage of couples are constantly at risk, because the man or woman is a carrier of a chromosome rearrangement. It is possible that there are also two classes of women whose miscarriages are caused by LPD. For the majority it is an occasional condition. A small percentage of women have LPD as a chronic condition, causing recurrent miscarriage. It may be that LPD is a normal part of our biology, another once-in-a-while-bad-luck condition leading to miscarriage.

LPD is considered an endocrine problem because it is traced to abnormalities in the production of, or response to, hormones. LPD is often defined (and treated) as the lack of adequate levels of progesterone to specialize and maintain the uterine lining for implantation. The average level of progesterone during the luteal phase is lower in groups of women with recurrent miscarriages than in groups of normally fertile women. The comparisons of progesterone levels are made during nonconceiving menstrual cycles between women who have had only successful pregnancies and women who have had only unsuccessful pregnancies.

In one study comparing the progesterone levels of fifteen such fertile women with progesterone levels of ten women with recurrent miscarriages, a clear difference was seen through much of the luteal phase, especially from days 4 to 11 after ovulation. Even though individual variations in the fertile group were wide, the lowest progesterone level in the fertile group was always higher than the highest level in the miscarriage group. For example, on day 8 after ovulation, the fertile group ranged from 9 to 18 nanograms of progesterone per milliliter of serum. The miscarriage group ranged from 4 to 6 nanograms per milliliter. This suggests that low luteal phase progesterone levels are definitely associated with miscarriage. But measuring progesterone levels in an individual may be misleading. On day 8, within a three-hour interval, the progesterone level can range from 6 to 35 nanograms per milliliter. So a few random samples in an individual are not sufficient by themselves to diagnose LPD.

Recall that the menstrual cycle is divided into two phases with reference to the ovaries. The time before ovulation is the follicular phase, named for the follicle, the nest of cells that holds the egg. Before ovulation, certain follicle cells release estrogen. The time after ovulation is the luteal phase (figure 1). After ovulation the empty follicle becomes a corpus luteum and makes more estrogen, as well as progesterone. Progesterone stimulates the uterine endometrium to secrete substances that help an embryo survive and implant.

It has been shown that if the corpus luteum is removed any time before 7 weeks after the last period, there will be a decrease in progesterone levels in the bloodstream, and then a miscarriage will occur. If a woman has to have her ovaries removed for some reason at this early stage, a miscarriage can be prevented by giving her progesterone supplements. This shows that progesterone is necessary for maintenance of early pregnancy and that its absence causes miscarriage. After 7 weeks, the placenta makes progesterone and the pregnancy begins to lose its dependence on the ovarian supply.

Another example illustrating the importance of progesterone is a birth control pill widely used in Europe, RU486. RU486 is a nonsteroid chemical imitator of progesterone with only some of progesterone's characteristics. RU486 enters cells and ties up the receptors that are required for a response to progesterone. RU486 makes these receptors unavailable, so that to the target cell, progesterone is not there. If RU486 is given during the luteal phase, a menstrual period will start within a few days. The uterus acts as though progesterone is gone.

While LPD is often defined as progesterone deficiency, this is not completely correct. LPD is the resulting condition in the uterus, the failure of the uterus to develop or sustain a good secretory endometrium. Many obstetricians agree that LPD is a cause of early miscarriage but that it cannot be blamed for mis-

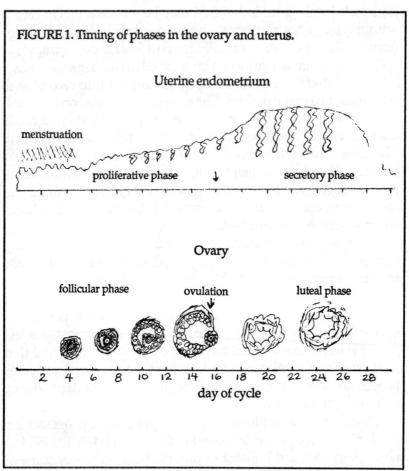

FIGURE 1. Timing of phases in the ovary and uterus.

Uterine endometrium

menstruation

proliferative phase   secretory phase

Ovary

follicular phase   ovulation   luteal phase

2 4 6 8 10 12 14 16 18 20 22 24 26 28

day of cycle

carriages occurring after 10 weeks, possibly none after 8 weeks. LPD is thought to be responsible for very early miscarriages, especially those occurring between 3 and 7 weeks after the last period. The earliest of these may go undetected and cause no delay in the menstrual period. Thus it is possible for a woman to think she cannot get pregnant when she is actually losing young embryos because of LPD.

Although many obstetricians agree that LPD is a primary or contributing factor to early miscarriage, it is a difficult condition to diagnose. As we will discuss later, many physicians treat suspected LPD with vaginal progesterone suppositories. Often such treatment is given to women who have had recurrent miscarriages, without doing any tests for LPD. LPD may also be treated with the fertility drug clomiphene (Clomid), with HCG, or even with HMG (Pergonal). Some obstetricians do not believe in giving excess hormones of any kind to a pregnant woman unless they are shown to be absolutely necessary.

Diagnosis of LPD is imperfect. Different physicians use different tests because of costs, convenience, available resources, and opinions on reliability. One routine way to diagnose LPD is by measurement of progesterone levels taken from blood samples. To measure progesterone levels, one must first determine the day of ovulation by following the basal body temperature (BBT). Usually progesterone is measured about 7 days after the BBT rise signals ovulation. This is about 8 days before the next period is due.

Progesterone levels range widely over the course of the day. To get around these changing levels, specialists recommend that three blood samples be taken, about an hour apart. The amount of progesterone is determined from the pooled samples. In practice the progesterone level is usually determined from a single sample. The amount of progesterone can be expressed as concentration, the amount in a volume of blood. The normal peak output of progesterone from the corpus luteum gives an average concentration of about 15 nanograms of progesterone per milliliter of serum. LPD is often defined as less than 15 nanograms per milliliter.

An alternative definition of LPD is a short luteal phase. The BBT chart can give evidence of this. LPD is suspected if, by following the temperature rise at ovulation, it is determined that the luteal phase of the cycle lasts less than 11 days. According to the medical literature, the most reliable diagnosis of LPD is made by studying the microscopic anatomy of the uterine endometrium during the secretory phase and finding it underdeveloped compared to normal. This is done by a technique called endometrial biopsy.

A biopsy is a small sample of tissue taken from an organ and analyzed in a laboratory. In the case of LPD, the tissue is studied carefully under the microscope to see if it looks like normal uterine endometrium. But the endometrium changes greatly in appearance over the course of a menstrual cycle and during pregnancy. To detect LPD, the endometrium must be sampled during the height of the luteal phase (secretory phase in the uterus) to see if the tissue is maximally developed, with proper organization and specialization.

An endometrial biopsy is never done during pregnancy. Some obstetricians will perform a very sensitive HCG test to be sure their patient is not in the early part of pregnancy. Then the uterine lining is gently scraped a few days before the ne xt period is due. Timing is very important, because the dating is only reliable in the last few days of the cycle. Many obstetricians will have their patient keep a careful BBT chart to determine the day of ovulation. This allows for more exact timing of the sample.

A pathologist is a specialist in the appearance of different types of organs and tissues. A pathologist experienced in endometrial dating must look at the sample and give it a date. This is a textbook date, based on the age of the endometrium compared to many samples taken from known times in the cycle For example, the test sample may be closest in appearance to a standard endometrium found 4 days before the period starts (4 days prior to menses). Then the patient must note the day her period actually starts.

The strictest definition of LPD is an endometrium that looks three days less developed than it should be. So if the tissue sample is judged to be 4 days prior to menses, but the period starts the next day, it was actually 1 day prior to menses. Thus it lags, is out of phase, by three days.

The other crucial part of an LPD diagnosis is that the lag in endometrial maturity must occur in two cycles in a row, not just one. The strictest definition of LPD as a chronic condition is at least a three-day lag in at least two cycles in a row. Physicians using one cycle of lagging development may over-diagnose the condition. However, for women with recurrent miscarriages, a single lagging endometrial sample is often considered justification for treatment. As I have said, physicians often treat recurrent miscarriages with progesterone without performing any tests.

The results of an endometrial biopsy are difficult to interpret because there are several places for error. The tissue sample must be taken within three days of the next period and it must be scraped from the fundus of the uterus, which is the highest point, the top of the uterus. The pathologist must be very experienced in reading this particular kind of tissue.

Theoretically, LPD is a direct result of decreased progesterone production by the corpus luteum, but there are many possible causes for that underproduction. Anything that upsets the timing of hormone release or the delicate balance of hormone levels can prevent the proper sequence of events in the menstrual cycle. Conditions affecting the brain, the pituitary, the ovaries, or the uterus can give the same ultimate result. Most evidence suggests that the root cause of LPD occurs before ovulation. LPD is considered a possibility in women with unexplained infertility, women who have recurrent miscarriages, and women whose BBT charts show they have a short luteal phase.

As we saw in chapter 7, estrogen made before ovulation causes the uterine endometrium to thicken. When referring to the uterus, this time is called the proliferative phase. Usually estrogen deficiency is not considered a cause of miscarriage. But estrogen is responsible for priming the cells of the endometrium to respond to progesterone. So if there is not enough estrogen during the first half of the cycle, the endometrium may not respond well to progesterone in the second half. Estrogen also acts on the follicle in the ovary. Together with the gonadotropin FSH, estrogen primes the follicle to respond to LH. LH is the main stimulant of progesterone secretion. Thus a shortage of estrogen during the follicular phase could result in underproduction of progesterone during the luteal phase. Shortages or imbalances in LH or FSH could have the same effect.

For there to be a good secretory endometrium, there must be enough progesterone made by the corpus luteum during the 10 days after ovulation. The uterus must respond properly to the progesterone. If the uterus is adequately prepared for an embryo to develop and implant properly, HCG will be made, which takes over from the pituitary to stimulate progesterone production.

A secondary kind of LPD can occur if HCG does not rescue the corpus luteum in time. Once ovulation occurs, the timing of events in the luteal phase becomes crucial. Progesterone levels rise for about 10 days. Then the corpus luteum begins an almost overnight degeneration. The only way to prevent this is for the embryo to arrive in the uterus, implant, and begin secreting HCG. The corpus luteum is saved within a day or two of its demise. Degeneration begins about 9 to 11 days after ovulation (figure 2). If an egg is fertilized on the day of ovulation and implants between days 6 and 7 after ovulation, it will begin making HCG by day 9. The corpus luteum will be saved.

But what about an egg fertilized on day 1 after ovulation? This embryo will not begin making HCG until day 10. Will enough be made in time to save the corpus luteum? If HCG does not arrive in time, progesterone levels will fall and miscarriage will result. It will be as if the pregnancy was not recognized by the ovary. Perhaps the quick degeneration of the corpus luteum is an adaptation that prevents development of borderline embryos, those made from eggs fertilized at the very last moment.

In the medical literature, LPD is considered the cause of miscarriage in between one out of four to two out of three women who have recurrent miscarriages. LPD is considered a possibility in a number of situations where the normal balance of hormones is upset. This is because the many different hormones we make, in various organs, are all directly or indirectly controlled by one part of the brain and the tiny pituitary gland. Sometimes large amounts of one hormone will affect the production of other hormones by acting on the brain. Thus LPD may occur in women who have taken various hormone supplements, including those used to induce ovulation. This is an unfortunate possibility, because the hormone treatment that allows pregnancy to begin may in turn cause a miscarriage.

Otherwise healthy women can also have hormone deficiencies or imbalances, and must consider the possibility of LPD. This includes those at either reproductive extreme: very young women who have just begun menstruation cycles, and women approaching the beginning of menopause. It includes women

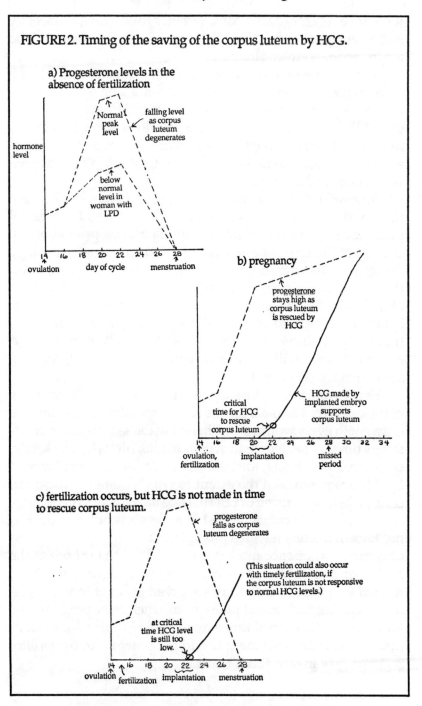

FIGURE 2. Timing of the saving of the corpus luteum by HCG.

a) Progesterone levels in the absence of fertilization

b) pregnancy

c) fertilization occurs, but HCG is not made in time to rescue corpus luteum.

who have recently had a baby, recently miscarried, or recently had a therapeutic abortion. LPD may also arise in women who are in vigorous athletic training.

LPD is one of the first possibilities considered when a woman has recurrent miscarriages. After a single miscarriage, LPD could be considered a possible cause if the woman falls into one of the categories just named, especially if she is over thirty-five and if the miscarriage was very early, before 8 weeks. However, most obstetricians will not test or treat for LPD in women with a single miscarriage.

In several studies it has been shown that women who have no reported fertility problems, and who have had successful pregnancies, have out-of-phase endometrial biopsies about 30 percent of the time. Specialists in reproductive endocrinology disagree on the significance of such results. They could mean that endometrial biopsies are interpreted incorrectly 30 percent of the time. They could mean that an out-of-phase endometrium is not an obstacle to successful pregnancy. They could mean that in approximately three out of every ten months, if an embryo forms it will not be able to find a receptive uterus, and a miscarriage will result.

Every woman may be subject to LPD as an occasional cause of miscarriage. The basis for the single episodes of LPD may be different in every woman, or different in the same woman at different times. The degree to which habits, lifestyle, workstyle, emotional well-being, and the like can affect the incidence of LPD is unknown, and the extent to which changing these can contribute to self curing of LPD may be impossible to determine.

The range of normal progesterone levels is rather wide. It is not known if women with a progesterone level at the lower end of normal experience more months of LPD than those at the higher end of normal. In some cases, women who are being treated for primary infertility are given progesterone supplements during their luteal phase even when their progesterone levels are in the normal range, without any testing for LPD. In many practices it is standard to add progesterone to the fertility regimen "just in case. It can't hurt."

Treatment for suspected or well-documented LPD is usually progesterone suppositories (vaginal) twice a day from the second or third day of the rise in BBT until the next period starts, or until the tenth week of pregnancy. In the 1960s a study was performed in which women with recurrent miscarriages were given either progesterone or inactive suppositories (placebos). There was no difference in the pregnancy success rates of the two groups. No similar controlled studies have been done since that time.

Using women with recurrent miscarriages as their own controls, progesterone supplements lead to 70 to 80 percent success in the next pregnancy. Yet there seem to have been no studies to determine if the progesterone supplements actually raise the circulating progesterone levels to normal.

Progesterone supplements do seem to prolong the luteal phase, which normally ends with a period when the corpus luteum degenerates and progesterone levels fall. With an external source of progesterone, the period will be late, even though there is no pregnancy. This can be demoralizing. The excess progesterone does not sustain the corpus luteum forever, and a period does finally arrive.

LPD may also be treated with clomiphene during the follicular phase. The increased levels of LH, FSH, and estrogen provide for higher progesterone in the luteal phase. Clomiphene is taken orally for five days, beginning on the second to fifth day of the cycle. Some obstetricians treat LPD with both clomiphene and progesterone. Clomiphene is given during the follicular phase and progesterone during the luteal phase. This regimen is also followed for women who have not been able to get pregnant. Often obstetricians prescribing clomiphene say it "gives you a push" or "improves the quality of eggs."

Much less often, HMG is used. HMG stands for Human Menopausal Gonadotropins (sold as Pergonal), which is a combination of FSH and LH. HMG is usually given to induce ovulation but is thought to help the luteal phase as well, for the same reasons as clomiphene. HMG must not be given without carefully monitoring the woman's estrogen levels or her ovaries (by ultrasound). This is because HMG can cause overstimulation of the ovaries, resulting in painful ovarian cysts or multiple births.

There are two general kinds of LPD. The more common is that caused by low progesterone levels. Less common is that caused by poor delivery of or response to normal levels of progesterone. As we have seen, the first group includes a wide range of women with abnormal hormonal or physiological conditions resulting in lower progesterone production. The second group includes women with uterine abnormalities that hinder circulation in the endometrium.

These abnormalities will be discussed in chapter 11. The most common example is the anatomical abnormality called septate uterus. Because of the altered shape and space in the uterus, circulation of blood is impaired. The result is that the amount of progesterone delivered to the endometrium is smaller than normal. This may be a local effect, depending on the exact spot in the uterus that implantation occurs. In that case there will be occasional, not chronic LPD. In one study, women with septate uterus and histories of miscarriages and no successful pregnancies were treated with progesterone suppositories during their next pregnancy, and 60 percent had successful pregnancies. This sounds impressive, but an uncontrolled study is not medically significant, since at least 40 percent of women with recurrent miscarriages have successful pregnancies without treatment. Endometrial biopsies were not performed on the women in the study.

Conditions of general health and well-being can affect pituitary function. Malnutrition, overexertion, and stress can probably cause or contribute to LPD. For example, women in training, who were running at least twenty miles a week throughout the month, had their cycles analyzed and compared to nontraining cycles. In both cases their cycle lengths were the same, and they had BBT charts that showed they were probably ovulating. Their temperatures went from lower to higher, and the higher temperature was sustained until their periods started. But during the training cycles their daily average progesterone levels were lower, and their luteal phases were shorter, than in their non-training cycles.

Some obstetricians think that in vitro fertilization patients have higher miscarriage rates than other women. Many others believe that there is no difference and that the apparently higher rate is caused by the awareness of pregnancy in the IVF patient. A possible cause of LPD in IVF patients is the loss of cells or fluids from the follicles when eggs are removed by aspiration with a needle and syringe. It is also possible that the stress of surgery and high levels of estrogen might cause hyperprolactinemia, an over-production of the milk-stimulating hormone prolactin.

Prolactin is a pituitary hormone that stimulates secretion of milk by mammary glands in the breasts. It is known that nursing mothers have moderate infertility. Very high levels of prolactin can cause primary infertility, while lower levels are thought to cause LPD. The reason is that prolactin acts on the brain, which influences the pituitary. Prolactin may also act on the ovaries to directly inhibit estrogen and progesterone secretion. In one study, one out of six women with diagnosed LPD had high prolactin levels. The treatment for hyperprolactinemia is a drug called bromocriptine. Bromocriptine acts by inhibiting the release of prolactin by the pituitary gland.

Rarely, hyperprolactinemia arises from a pituitary tumor. Also rarely, it arises from another abnormal hormone condition, hypothyroidism. Hypothyroidism is underproduction of thyroid hormone. In this case the LPD can be cured by thyroid hormone supplements. Although hypothyroidism is not common, it is easy to diagnose and treat.

With all the complex signaling traffic going to and from the pituitary, it is not surprising that unusually large amounts of one factor or hormone may sometimes stimulate or inhibit the wrong hormone. Thus when a person has abnormally low thyroid hormone levels, the brain keeps stimulating the pituitary to stimulate the thyroid gland. This accidentally stimulates the pituitary to release the wrong hormone, prolactin. Prolactin secretion can be increased by various abnormal triggers of the nerves that are normally stimulated by nursing. For example, stimulation of these nerves can come from infection by Herpes zoster virus, certain drugs, trauma, physical damage to the spine, and kidney disease.

Another rare hormonal abnormality is hyperandrogenemia. This refers to abnormally high levels of androgens, male sex hormones, which women normally make at very low levels. Most studies of recurrent miscarriages do not take into account the possibility of excessive amounts of androgens. However, it has been shown in laboratory studies that testosterone can inhibit progesterone production by the corpus luteum.

One particular androgen associated with LPD in some women is called DHEA-S. In one group of twelve women with LPD who did not succeed in pregnancy after treatment with either progesterone or clomiphene, four of the twelve had elevated levels of the androgen DHEA-S. Three of these four had successful pregnancies after treatment with a drug that reduces the androgen levels (dexamethasone). The drug was given before, rather than during, pregnancy.

Ovulation and fertilization are required for conception, but they are not the only requirements for early pregnancy to succeed. Growth and specialization of the uterine endometrium is vital to establishing and maintaining the early embryo and allowing further development of the placenta. LPD is a condition in which the uterus fails in its early preparation.

A possible advantage to our species for the occurrence of LPD is to increase the spacing of births, so that each child is parented longer when small. This was more important for survival when we were wandering hunter-gatherers 50,000 years ago. But our biology has not had time to evolve much since then. Occasional LPD would compensate for our year-round fertility. Support for this notion is that one group of women often found to have LPD are those who have recently given birth. It is also known that nursing mothers may have reduced fertility through the action of prolactin.

Beginning with the brain and pituitary, the sequence of events that must all work properly to maintain early pregnancy is at least as complicated as to get pregnancy started. There are many steps in a complex chain of signals and responses required for a healthy luteal phase. There are many possible sources of disturbance for each. If a woman has kept a calendar of her menstrual cycles, she may want to check back and try to remember any obviously late periods. The more regular her cycles are, the easier this will be. The miscarriage she has experienced may not be the only one she has had. If she has a strong suspicion that she has had more than one very early miscarriage, she may wish to discuss it with her obstetrician. It is not certain that LPD is treatable, though many doctors treat it. It is not easy to agree on a diagnosis. But it is clear that luteal phase deficiency usually causes miscarriage before ultrasound can show that a pregnancy is "going well."

Chapter 11

Other Causes of Miscarriage

Anatomic Abnormalities, Infection, and Immunologic Causes of Miscarriage

STUDIES OF THE NONGENETIC CAUSES OF MISCARRIAGE focus on recurrent miscarriages and may not necessarily explain a first or only miscarriage. In looking for nongenetic as well as genetic explanations for miscarriage, we must consider two categories: conditions unique to the pregnancy that miscarried, and chronic conditions, which can cause future miscarriages. In most cases miscarriage is caused by a one-time bad-luck occurrence. This may be a chromosomal defect, an inadequate luteal phase, or some multifactorial condition. If the same couple has a second miscarriage, it may not have the same cause as the first. In the case of single miscarriage not due to a chromosomal defect, it may be impossible to fully trace or explain the cause.

Much more rarely, a couple will have a series of miscarriages. Some men and women are carriers of abnormal chromosome arrangements. Every time they make sperm or eggs there is a very high chance of making certain chromosomal abnormalities. Some women have endocrine abnormalities that create chronic LPD (luteal phase deficiency) a condition that causes early miscarriage. In this chapter I will discuss three other nongenetic causes of miscarriage. First I will discuss physical abnormalities of the uterus; second, infections of the mother's reproductive tract; and third, abnormal immune responses to the embryo, including autoimmune conditions.

Uterine abnormalities, especially anatomic, are fairly uncommon, and do not usually cause miscarriage by themselves. Maternal infections are quite widespread, but among several organisms suspected of causing miscarriage, most cannot be shown to cause miscarriage by themselves. Certain autoimmune conditions are associated with miscarriage. Other abnormal immune responses in early pregnancy are theoretical and currently subjects of investigation and experimental therapy. In each case I will explain how a particular condition can be diagnosed and treated, and whether obstetricians think that treatment actually reduces the chances of miscarriage. For some conditions there is no reliable treatment.

A. Uterine Abnormalities.

Abnormal physical conditions of the uterus include anatomical defects present at birth, cervical incompetence (a cervix that does not close up tightly enough to contain the large fetus and placenta), intrauterine adhesions (scar tissue in the walls of the uterus), and leiomyomas (fibroid tumors of the uterus). Physical problems of the uterus have a fairly straightforward but unpleasant means of diagnosis. The obstetrician must observe the contours and content of the uterus, either by X-ray techniques (hysterosalpingogram) or surgery (laparoscopy or hysteroscopy). Correction of such abnormalities, when it is possible, usually involves surgery.

One widely accepted anatomical cause of miscarriage is called a septate, or double, uterus. A *septum*, Latin for "fence" or "wall," divides the uterus into two halves. Depending on the condition causing the malformation, the septum may be partial or complete (figure 1). During development of the reproductive tract, the fetus first forms a pair of tubes. Each one begins near a developing ovary, and runs to the single excretory opening. The parts of each tube that lie near each ovary develop into each of the uterine tubes, the oviducts. The remaining central parts of the two tubes fuse, then enlarge and form into the uterus and vagina

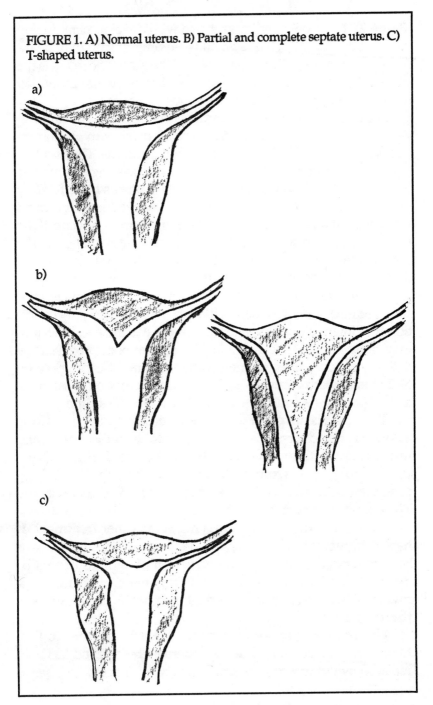

FIGURE 1. A) Normal uterus. B) Partial and complete septate uterus. C) T-shaped uterus.

a)

b)

c)

(figure 2). If there is any interference with development during the time the reproductive system is shaping, fusion may be incomplete anywhere along the length of the tube. One result is the septate uterus. A septate uterus can be changed to an undivided uterus by a surgical technique called metroplasty.

Septate uterus is not a common condition. But among women who have recurrent miscarriages, those with uterine abnormalities are most likely to have a septate uterus. Thus septate uterus may contribute to the incidence of miscarriage. However, only one out of five women with septate uterus have fertility problems of any kind. Having a septate uterus does not mean a woman must miscarry. It is thought that miscarriage occurs if the embryo tries to implant in the septum itself. Implantation in the normal part of the uterus may or may not pose problems, depending on the exact location and the extent of the septum.

Septate uterus can be associated with early miscarriage, possibly because of poor blood circulation in the uterus. Any condition that interferes with circulation in the uterine endometrium may cause luteal phase deficiency because of poor progesterone delivery . In one study, women with recurrent miscarriages who had septate uterus were treated with progesterone suppositories, and 60 percent had successful pregnancies the next time.

This result is not proof that the women had LPD, but, as long as there is no adverse effect of progesterone on the developing fetus, this treatment is worth trying before doing surgery. Presumably the women who were helped by taking progesterone would need to take it every time they get pregnant. The women in the group who were not helped by progesterone have the difficult decision of trying some other treatment or having surgery. In one review of the medical literature, it was recommended that surgical correction of septate uterus be delayed until first ruling out LPD, genetic abnormalities, mycoplasma infection and cervical incompetence as causes of the miscarriage.

Until recently, major abdominal surgery was the surgical treatment for women with septate uterus. This method has been replaced by hysteroscopic surgery, where instruments are inserted

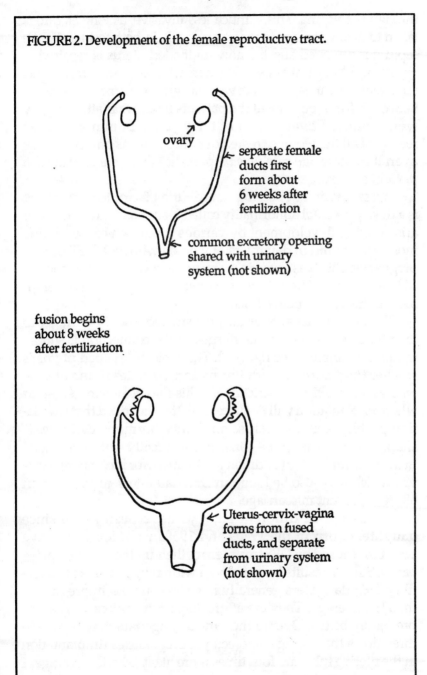

FIGURE 2. Development of the female reproductive tract.

ovary

separate female ducts first form about 6 weeks after fertilization

common excretory opening shared with urinary system (not shown)

fusion begins about 8 weeks after fertilization

Uterus-cervix-vagina forms from fused ducts, and separate from urinary system (not shown) through the vagina. This is much less invasive, as long as care is taken to avoid damage to the uterine wall. In both techniques the septum is removed and the now undivided uterus is repaired.

In one hospital where women with septate uterus and recurrent miscarriages underwent surgical treatment, the numbers of children born to all the patients before and after surgery were collected over a span of forty years. Summing up the results of all the women treated over the years as one group, the overall miscarriage rate was 95 percent before surgery and 18 percent after surgery.

A less certain but possible contributing factor to miscarriage is a developmental abnormality called T-shaped uterus. This can arise during development by various unknown causes, but is most often found in daughters of women who took DES during pregnancy. DES was given to many women who threatened miscarriage in the 1950s. It is now known to interfere with development of the reproductive tract.

The uterine tubes are usually constricted, and the entrance to the uterus is narrow, so the uterus-to-tube connection is square rather than angled (see figure 1). The typical T-shaped uterus is smaller than normal, with lumps and wrinkles in the uterine wall called "cavity constrictions." This may leave limited areas where implantation will be successful. It is theorized that circulation problems in the uterus can reduce hormone delivery. T-shaped uterus cannot be corrected surgically. Often hormone treatments for LPD, in addition to treatment for incompetent cervix, which may also be found in DES daughters, are used in an effort to prevent miscarriage.

A number of different surveys have been made since daughters born in the 1940s and 1950s were found to have problems caused by DES treatment of their mothers during pregnancy. Survey results have found a wide range of effects on fertility. DES daughters generally have less success in pregnancy than the average. They are at greater risk for miscarriages and premature births. Overall their miscarriage rate may be two to three times the average, and ectopic pregnancies (implantation in the uterine tube) are four times more likely than the average, 1 percent. The earlier in her pregnancy the mother took DES, the more severe the uterine abnormality in her daughter, because the reproductive system forms before 12 weeks.

About two out of three DES daughters have uterine abnormalities, but most still have successful pregnancies. Incompetent cervix is one of the most common and severe problems of DES daughters. It is also usually their only treatable anatomical condition. I will discuss incompetent cervix further on.

An obstetrician will usually order a hysterosalpingogram as part of the series of evaluations of a woman with recurrent miscarriages (as well as women with primary infertility). If a woman knows her mother took DES, such a test may be performed earlier in the series. The hysterosalpingogram requires injection of iodine dye solution into the uterus, and may be rather uncomfortable. If a woman's uterus is very deformed, the dye may not be easily taken up. Then an X ray is taken, and the dye lights up all the nooks and crannies in the uterus and tubes.

Not every feature of uterine anatomy is revealed by the hysterogram, so laparoscopy may be required. The laparoscope is a long instrument that carries a little light into the abdominal cavity. At the upper, outside end of it is an eyepiece through which the surgeon views the inside, somewhat like looking through a telescope. The laparoscope is introduced through an incision in the navel. Then surgical instruments can be introduced through lower incisions. Small incisions are made, and the whole operation can be viewed on a video screen. The uterus, tubes, and ovaries can be seen, and surgical repair can be performed. Scar tissue and misplaced endometrial tissue, as in endometriosis, can be removed. Laparoscopy was used to harvest eggs from ovaries for in vitro fertilization, though it has been replaced by the simpler use of a needle guided by ultrasound. Laparoscopy is also used to remove ectopic embryos from uterine tubes.

A newer surgical technique is hysteroscopy. Here the surgical instruments are introduced through the vagina. Uterine surgery can include reconstruction of a septate uterus and removal of intrauterine tumors or scar tissue. Any surgery must be undertaken with a clear understanding of what it can and cannot accomplish, as well as the risks. For example, surgery involving the uterine tubes may increase the risk of ectopic pregnancy. New scar tissue from the surgery can interfere with pregnancy. Uterine surgery is never guaranteed to restore fertility or remove the threat of miscarriage. Women with uterine abnormalities may have other problems that contribute to their infertility. On the other hand, there are many women with uterine abnormalities who do not have any fertility problems.

A widely accepted cause of miscarriage is incompetent cervix. This condition may only be blamed for miscarriages that occur after at least 12 weeks, usually 16 weeks or later. Normally the long cervix is tightly constricted during pregnancy. During delivery the progress of labor is measured by the width of expansion (dilation) of the cervix. Some women will miscarry because their cervix dilates long ahead of schedule due to weakness of its tissues. Often these women have an anatomical problem, including a shallow uterus with short cervix. Incompetent cervix is often found in women with other uterine abnormalities. It can sometimes be diagnosed by hysterogram, ultrasound, or more recently MRI scans (magnetic resonance imaging). The finding that a cervical dilating instrument of a particular diameter (#8 Hegar dilator) passes easily through the nonpregnant cervix is also diagnostic of cervical incompetence.

DES daughters seem to have a high incidence of incompetent cervix. Incompetent cervix is generally not considered unless there is a history of late miscarriages, the woman's mother took DES, or a checkup during the second trimester of pregnancy finds a dilated cervix. Miscarriage due to incompetent cervix can be prevented by a surgical procedure called cerclage, where the cervix is cinched up like a string pouch. The woman is advised to curtail her activities, and sometimes takes a modified form of progesterone (sold as Delalutin) to prevent preterm labor. Usually cerclage is performed between the 12th and 15th week so that it does not prevent an early miscarriage from other causes, such as genetic defects, from going to completion. The sutures are removed at 37 weeks to allow delivery of the baby at term, or left in place and the baby delivered by Caesarian section.

Fibroid tumors, called leiomyomas, are benign growths in the uterus. Depending on their size, they may interfere with uterine blood flow and endometrial growth, or hinder implantation. Such growths can be removed by hysteroscopic or abdominal surgery in an operation called myomectomy. Intrauterine adhesions, also called Asherman's syndrome, are considered by some but not all obstetricians to contribute to miscarriage. The size of the uterine cavity can be reduced by adhesions, because their connections to the walls pull them closer together. The ability of the uterine cavity to expand during pregnancy is also reduced. In addition, circulation may be poor, and the endometrium may not develop well. Asherman's syndrome appears to result from multiple causes, including trauma from surgery or infection. Some obstetricians think that the adhesions may be the result of recurrent miscarriages, where some of the fetal and placental tissues are left in the uterus. The uterus has an inflammatory response to the tissues, and fibrous adhesions result.

A summary of five independent studies of women with intrauterine adhesions concluded that removal of adhesive tissue using hysteroscopy reduced the miscarriage rate from 67 percent to 26 percent. These were all studies using the women as their own controls. The number of pregnancies and miscarriages the women had before surgery was compared to the number after surgery.

Another uterine abnormality is called endometriosis. This is a condition where the tissue specific to the uterine endometrium starts growing outside of the uterus. It causes irregular and painful menstrual periods. There is disagreement among obstetricians whether endometriosis contributes to the incidence of miscarriage. It is more commonly associated with primary infertility. In one study of a small group of women with endometriosis who had recurrent miscarriages, the incidence of miscarriage was reduced after hysteroscopic surgery to remove the extraneous tissue.

B. Maternal Infections.

There is an association between certain infections of women's reproductive tracts and miscarriage, but a definite cause and effect relationship has not been shown. A variety of infectious microorganisms are found in pregnant women, some in higher proportions of women who miscarry than in women who do not. Information is unavailable about specific strains of each organism and the particular location of infection that may be responsible for killing an embryo or for inducing very premature labor.

There is disagreement among obstetricians about the role that infections of the mother's reproductive tract play in miscarriage. No thorough studies have been made of all the infectious agents—bacteria, viruses, and others—that grow in the vagina, uterus, and possibly fetal or placental tissues. No one has ever followed the occurrence of any of these infections over the reproductive lifetime of a group of women. Maternal infections often may be treated with antibiotics, but obstetricians disagree about the necessity for treatment.

People often think of bacteria as disease-causing "germs." Though there are certainly many notorious bacterial agents of disease, there are also many microorganisms that live harmlessly in, on, and around us. Our lower digestive system is laden with bacteria, as are our skin, and lower reproductive tract. There are also micro-organisms not usually found in these places that can cause mild to severe disorders when they do grow there. Sometimes an infectious agent that does little harm to a woman may severely damage an embryo. Consider the case of rubella, the German measles virus. The virus gives children or adults an unpleasant but rarely life-threatening rash and fever. Yet it severely deforms, even kills, a developing fetus. Pregnant women are usually checked to see if they have had rubella in the past. If not they are advised to avoid large gatherings of children. Women who are not pregnant can be given a vaccination against it.

In order to go unrecognized, an infectious agent that can cause miscarriage must be one that does not make the mother very ill. If it does, she will seek treatment or mount a strong immune response and remove the infectious agent from her body.

The various agents thought to contribute to miscarriage are generally considered to cause infections that are asymptomatic, that is, have no obvious symptoms. Yet some women report a fever during pregnancies that end in miscarriage, and they also test positive for microorganisms such as mycoplasma. Others who miscarry and test positive for such infectious agents report they have severe fatigue during the pregnancy. This may be hard to distinguish from normal pregnancy tiredness without a previous uninfected pregnancy to compare it to.

Infections of the vagina generally do not reach the uterus or uterine tubes, thanks to the protective barrier of the cervical tunnel and the viscous mucus that is present except for the days around ovulation. However, the string of an IUD can act as a wick to assist the movement of infectious agents from the vagina to the uterus. That is the reason that women who use IUDs are at greater risk for infections of the uterus and fallopian tubes, which may lead to scarring and reduced fertility. There is also evidence that some infectious agents can attach to the tails of sperm, and travel with them into the upper parts of a woman's reproductive tract. Viruses, toxoplasma, and mycoplasma are found to travel this way. In humans the sperm tail enters the egg and may be a means of infecting the embryo.

Four micro-organisms that are considered possible causes of miscarriage are listeria, toxoplasma, mycoplasma, and chlamydia. Listeria and toxoplasma are transmitted through either food or hand-to-mouth contact. Mycoplasma and chlamydia are transmitted sexually, and because of this are more prevalent in women, yet less certain as causes of miscarriage.

Listeria is a bacterium that grows in milk products such as cheese. A woman must eat contaminated foods to become infected. Listeria is not routinely identified in cultures from women. A laboratory must look for it specifically. Listeria infections are often asymptomatic, but are considered fatal to the fetus and even to newborns. It can be treated with penicillin-related antibiotics. It is not considered a likely cause of recurrent miscarriages but may be responsible for isolated events of fetal death. A woman would have had to eat contaminated milk products before or early in her pregnancy to suspect listeria as the cause.

Toxoplasma is a parasite found in uncooked meat. It is common in underdeveloped parts of the world and is also found in cats, thus in cat litter. There may be no symptoms of infection, and so it must be specifically tested for biochemically. Toxoplasma causes severe birth defects, especially brain defects, and seems to be an uncommon cause of miscarriage.

Mycoplasma is the smallest living cell. It is closely related to bacteria but simpler in structure. There are two kinds of mycoplasma associated with miscarriage. One has the scientific name Mycoplasma hominis, and the other, Ureaplasma urealyticum. I will refer to them both as mycoplasma. Vaginal mycoplasma infections alone do not appear to cause miscarriage, but their presence in pregnant women is associated with a greater risk of miscarriage.

Placental and fetal tissues are found to be infected with mycoplasma six to ten times more often in miscarried tissues than in aborted tissues. It can be argued that pregnancies that are failing for other reasons are more susceptible to infection. Some obstetricians believe that the infection can only cause miscarriage if it gets into the uterine endometrium. Endometrial tissues were cultured from women with recurrent miscarriages and from women with only normal pregnancies. Mycoplasma was detected in the endometrium of 20 percent of the women with recurrent miscarriages but only 7 percent of the women with only normal pregnancies. These findings suggest an association between mycoplasma and miscarriage but not an absolute cause-and-effect relationship.

In one study of women with recurrent miscarriages who had mycoplasma, the women and their husbands were treated with antibiotics before their next pregnancy. 90 percent had successful pregnancies the next time. Depending on the study, mycoplasma is found in the cervical cultures of about 50 percent of pregnant women. Because of this, obstetricians do not take such infections seriously as the cause of miscarriage. They will usually not test for or treat such infections until a woman has had three miscarriages.

When specific strains of mycoplasma are identified, one particular strain (called serotype 3) is found more often in women with fertility problems, while a different strain is found more often in fertile women. Thus, when obstetricians consider mycoplasma infection to be unimportant in miscarriage, they are generalizing from studies that are not specific enough. It is very likely that mycoplasma infection is a contributing, rather than primary, cause of miscarriage, but this is impossible to demonstrate.

Chlamydia is a bacterium that has been implicated in miscarriage, although it is more often considered to damage uterine tubes and cause infertility. Although many practicing obstetricians do not believe that mycoplasma or chlamydia cause miscarriage, they will prescribe antibiotics to their patients with recurrent miscarriages who have evidence of cervical infection.

Various viruses are suspected of causing miscarriage, if they actually infect the fetal tissues or placenta, but except for HSV-2 (Herpes simplex virus type 2), which is very common in the reproductive tract, there is no treatment. HSV-2 can be treated with the drug acyclovir. Though HSV-2 is common in the lower reproductive tract, it does not seem to pose a problem unless it gets into the uterine endometrium.

It would be informative to study two large groups of women: those who have a particular infection, and those who do not. The women in both groups should be followed through several pregnancies, and any differences in the incidence of miscarriage could be determined. Studies of any single infectious agent would have to involve only that organism, but many women have more than one infection simultaneously.

C. Abnormal Immune Response.

Biologists have been studying the immune system for many years. Certain of our white blood cells, or lymphocytes, provide our immune defense against disease. Immunity depends on the ability to distinguish between substances or cells that are part of us, or "self," and those that are foreign, or "nonself." This function is carried out by proteins called antibodies that are highly specific in their recognition of other substances. We make many different antibodies and each one binds a single substance. The classic analogy is to a lock and key.

A substance that can stimulate an immune response is called an antigen. To stimulate the response an antigen must enter the body and then encounter a lymphocyte carrying the antibody specific to that antigen. Each lymphocyte carries a single kind of antibody. Binding of antigen to antibody on the lymphocyte stimulates that cell to divide many times, generating a population of like cells that produce large quantities of the specific antibody. Some antibodies circulate freely and some are carried on lymphocytes. When an antibody binds its specific antigen the antigen is inactivated. If the antigen is on a cell the cell is destroyed.

It takes time to develop an immune response to an antigen. Only after large quantities of antibody are produced can we inactivate large amounts of antigen. If a person is infected by a virus or other pathogen (disease-causing agent) the virus will multiply and cause disease symptoms until enough lymphocytes are producing enough specific antibody to destroy the virus. If the symptoms of infection are very serious, a person may die before the immune system can eliminate the virus.

After the first exposure to an antigen, the body sets aside a larger population of cells specific for that antigen than were originally present. These are called memory cells. If an antigen appears again months or years later the response is much bigger and faster. This is called a secondary response and is the basis for natural immunization. The person who survives the first infection by a particular virus will not become ill when exposed again, because this time enough antibodies are made right away to remove the virus before it multiplies. In artificial immunization, or vaccination, an inactivated form or a harmless fragment of the pathogen is used as an antigen, so the slow response of the first exposure does not endanger the person. If the person is later exposed to the active pathogen, the rapid and massive secondary response eliminates the pathogen before it can cause symptoms.

There are a variety of medical conditions and diseases that

are caused by malfunctions of the immune system. One kind of immune disorder is autoimmune disease, meaning an immune reaction against substances or cells that should be recognized as "self." A person with an autoimmune disease makes antibodies that destroy certain of his or her own tissues. Juvenile-onset diabetes, rheumatoid arthritis, multiple sclerosis, systemic lupus erythematosus (SLE), and other diseases result from autoimmune responses.

Women with the disease SLE have high rates of miscarriage, apparently through the action of the autoimmune antibody called lupus anticoagulant (LAC). It is thought that LAC damages the blood vessels in the uterus. LAC is found in some women who have no symptoms of SLE. For this reason women who have recurrent miscarriages are tested for the presence of LAC. In two studies women with LAC had a total of 354 miscarriages in 404 pregnancies, a miscarriage rate of 88 percent. More than one third of the pregnancy losses occurred after 13 weeks. Aspirin interferes with formation of clots that can block blood vessels, so it is given in low doses to reduce the risk of miscarriage in women with LAC. Steroids similar to those made by the adrenal gland may be given in addition to aspirin to suppress the immune response. In one study women with LAC who took low doses of aspirin and the steroid Prednisone during their next pregnancy had 70 percent of the pregnancies succeed.

When blood transfusion and later organ transplantation became medically possible, we learned that humans mount an immune response to cells from other humans. Cells in each individual have surface substances which differ slightly from cells in other individuals, and such surface substances act as antigens if introduced into another person. The family of antigens responsible for immune rejection of transplanted organs is called HLA, for Human Leukocyte Antigen (leukocyte is another word for white blood cell). There are several different HLA antigens, and each has a variety of specific forms in the population. We inherit specific HLA forms from our parents.

Because of the wide variety of HLA types it is very unlikely that two unrelated people will have any of the same HLA antigens. For this reason there are very few women who could accept organ transplants from their husbands. Biologists have long wondered why mothers do not reject their developing fetus as "nonself," since it must have some HLA or other surface antigens from its father. Somehow the mother allows the fetus to thrive in the uterus.

This is even more mysterious when we consider that there is a well-known case of maternal immune response against the fetus, Rh-incompatibility. Rh, for Rhesus factor, is an antigen found on the surface of red blood cells. People who are Rh-positive have this antigen while people who are Rh-negative do not have it. If an Rh-negative person is given Rh-positive blood cells, the person will be immunized to Rh factor. The next time this person receives Rh-positive blood large amounts of antibodies against the Rh antigen will be made. These can bind Rh-positive cells and destroy them. People who are Rh-positive do not have an immune response to Rh-negative blood.

The presence or absence of Rh factor is inherited. A man and woman who are both Rh-negative can only have Rh-negative children. If either parent, or both parents, is Rh-positive, their children may be Rh-positive or Rh-negative. If a woman is Rh-positive she does not have to worry whether her children are Rh-positive or Rh-negative.

If a woman is Rh-negative and her husband is Rh-positive they may have Rh-positive children. If the mother carries an Rh-positive fetus, she may be exposed to small numbers of fetal red blood cells that occasionally leak through breaks in small blood vessels in the placenta late in pregnancy and around birth. Her first baby is not in any danger, but the next time the woman carries an Rh-positive fetus, if any of its blood cells get into her system before its birth, she will have a secondary response, producing lots of Rh-specific antibody. Since antibodies are proteins they cross the placenta easily. The babies' red blood cells will be destroyed, resulting in severe anemia that can cause fetal or newborn death. Newborns can be saved by blood transfusions.

Rh-negative women who have been pregnant are familiar with a treatment now used to prevent them from becoming immunized against Rh factor. After miscarriage, abortion, or amniocentesis, at 28 weeks of pregnancy, and after delivery, Rh-negative women receive a shot called Rhogam. This is a preparation of antibodies from other people's blood that includes those specific for the Rh factor. The Rh-specific antibodies are in large enough amounts to find and bind any of the baby's Rh-positive cells that have entered the mother, somewhat like sponging up a spill, so the mother's lymphocytes never encounter them. The next pregnancy is equivalent to a first-time exposure to the Rh factor.

According to some studies of infertility, there are rare instances of a woman becoming immunized to her husband's sperm. She makes antibodies against sperm surface antigens and these antibodies destroy the sperm in the cervix. It was theorized that if these women became pregnant they might destroy the embryo with the same sperm-specific antibodies, but there is no convincing evidence that this is a cause of miscarriage. Instead there is something special about the embryo that keeps the mother from mounting an immune response to its paternal (father's) components.

There is now thought to be a special kind of immune response: a protective one. It is normal for the mother to recognize the embryo as "nonself," but the antibodies she makes are a special protective kind. Instead of destroying the embryo these protective antibodies shield it from the lymphocytes of her immune system. It is theorized that, in order for this protective response to work, there must be enough differences in cell surface markers, such as HLA antigens, between the mother and father so that the embryo carrying paternal markers will be recognized as "nonself." There are cases of women with unexplained recurrent early miscarriages who have two or more HLA antigens in common with their husbands. It is thought that, because of the similarities in the parents' cell surface antigens, the embryo looks too much like "self" to the mother's system and she does not make the protective immune response. The other components of her immune system respond and destroy the embryo.

Experimental treatment for this postulated condition attempts to enhance the mother's ability to recognize paternal cells as "nonself." She is immunized with her husband's lymphocytes. This is done through a series of injections over several months before her next pregnancy. As yet there is no definitive evidence that this is a real cause of miscarriage or that the treatment works. In one study 75 percent of the women with unexplained recurrent miscarriages who were immunized with their husbands' lymphocytes had success in the next pregnancy. In a group of in vitro fertilization patients, the rate of successful pregnancies increased from 30 percent to 50 percent after women were immunized with their husband's lymphocytes.

Such immune treatments sound very promising, but we should keep in mind that only a very small number of women can possibly have such problems. In addition, there are risks with such procedures, which involve many unknowns with regard to the contents of the man's cells and the woman's response. One obstetrician reported that several women who had been immunized with their husbands' cells gave birth to premature babies showing severe growth retardation. The immune response system is very complex and can malfunction in the direction of over-response or under-response. It is not certain how either kind of failure contributes to miscarriage.

There is much less certainty that some of the conditions discussed in this chapter cause miscarriage than there is about genetic causes. In most cases the absolute cause-and-effect relationship between the condition and miscarriage is not established. This means that a woman or her obstetrician may hesitate to undertake the expense and unpleasantness of diagnosis or treatment. This is especially true when we consider that many miscarriages are probably caused by the sum of several partially contributing factors. Eliminating one of the contributing factors may not remove the threat of future miscarriage. It may be worthwhile to focus on eliminating contributing factors that are easier to treat before taking on more difficult factors, such as those that require surgery or unknown risks.

Chapter 12

Miscarriage and Other Fertility Risks for Prospective Mothers Over 35

THERE ARE AT LEAST THREE MAJOR DIFFICULTIES FOR WOMEN who experience miscarriage. First is total shock, both physical and emotional. Miscarriage is not expected. Second is the feeling of isolation, when others do not understand how strong the sense of loss and the sadness can be after miscarriage. Miscarriage grief has not traditionally been acceptable. Third is the fear of infertility. Miscarriage is a failed pregnancy, and may be a sign of future failures.

In this chapter I will explain why prospective mothers over thirty-five should prepare themselves and expect to miscarry more often than younger women. I will also explain why they might feel especially deep sorrow, and why they must be aware of an increased risk of infertility. However, women over thirty five do have some advantages over younger women in dealing with these problems. Their maturity and experience in the world can give them more confidence in seeking other women to talk to and in asking question of their doctors. Their ability to make decisions can help them work through the choices they are facing.

It has become common popular knowledge that many women just starting their families in the 1990s are older than their own mothers were when they had their third or fourth child. Increasing social acceptance of women having careers, the increasing acceptance and ease of getting divorced, and other social phenomena have created a large population of women who were not ready or able to start having children as young as their mothers were. The availability of reliable birth control and the legalization of abortion have made it possible to prevent or terminate pregnancy. This has introduced a very clear factor of choice in family planning.

It is not that our parents did no family planning; only that their efforts were less certain, and for different purposes. Many of our parents used the rhythm method or condoms to approximately plan the spacing of their children, but these methods are inexact. During the post-World War II years it was not particularly acceptable for a couple to decide they did not want children, or even that they wanted to put off having children. In the 1950s, forty-year-old women were often thought of as middle-aged matrons.

An interesting complication has developed in current generations of prospective mothers. Just as women now have the ability to choose when and how many children to have, so do their men. This is really a men's liberation issue, and it is not often raised. Men have the opportunity to say, "Let's wait." In our parents' generation it was understood that people married and had children. In more recent generations people can and often have to debate and decide each step. Should we marry? Shall we have children? When should we have children? How many children should we have?

In addition to their own professional pursuits, general economic worries and an awareness of world overpopulation and environmental decline can contribute to a couple's delay in childbearing, especially if they wish their children to have the same quality of life that they had. At the time a woman and her husband are finally ready to start their family, both have often been in decision-making positions for many years. Now they begin the seemingly simple task of making babies. When a woman who has been in charge of her life has a miscarriage, the devastation she feels is compounded by this fall from a great height of command. Not only that, but the child of a couple in their late thirties has truly been planned, and often long awaited.

The couple may develop a strong attachment to the unborn child early in the pregnancy, so they feel their loss very deeply.

If, as part of their pregnancy preparations, they had learned that miscarriage was a very likely outcome, perhaps their feelings of failing and being out of control would be eased, even if only a little. If they began their effort to have a baby with a clear expectation of delays and setbacks, at least the losses would not take them totally by surprise. This is true for couples of any age, because miscarriage is always a possibility, but it is greater for couples over thirty-five. The chances of making eggs, and probably sperm, with chromosomal abnormalities increase with age. This is a very real effect and should be clearly understood as an obstacle to instant success by couples starting to have children in their late thirties.

If we consider the results of one survey, we can see how much chromosomal defects contribute to the incidence of miscarriage in women over thirty five, compared to women under thirty-five. In studies described in chapters 8 and 9, when chromosomal analysis was performed on miscarried tissues, the age and reproductive history of the mothers were recorded. From the numbers, we can determine the chances that a miscarriage was caused by chromosomal abnormalities, depending on the woman's age and whether she has miscarried before.

For women under thirty-five, the chances that the tissues from a first miscarriage will be found to have chromosomal abnormalities are about 40 percent. The tissues from a second miscarriage are somewhat less likely to have chromosomal abnormalities, 34 percent, and the third miscarriage for a woman under thirty five is much less likely to be due to chromosomal abnormalities, only 19 percent. In chapter 8 I described a separate study, not corrected for age, where third and fourth miscarriages were combined, and only 6 percent of these were due to chromosomal abnormalities. Recurrent miscarriages are generally due to non-genetic causes.

If we now consider results from the same study for women over thirty-five, we find that first, second, or third miscarriages have almost the same chances of being caused by chromosomal abnormalities, about 50 percent. In this particular study, 52 percent of the first miscarriages had chromosomal abnormalities, and 48 percent of the second and third miscarriages did. We should also keep in mind that the actual occurrence of chromosomal abnormalities is probably much higher than the level detected in tissues recovered from clinical pregnancies. So the chances for chromosomal defects are high enough that it can happen again and again, just by chance. As prospective mothers age, they have an increasing risk of recurrent miscarriages due to nothing but bad genetic luck.

Unfortunately, chromosomal abnormalities are not the only causes of miscarriage that increase with age. If we consider that the average time between puberty and menopause is thirty seven years, from the age of thirteen to fifty, it is quite clear that a forty-year-old is much closer to menopause than a thirty-year-old. Menopause is the time when the ovaries shut down production of hormones. It signals the end of fertility in women and is marked by a steep drop in estrogen production. Most of the unpleasant symptoms of menopause are caused by this loss of estrogen, and women often take estrogen supplements to reduce their occurrence. For example, hot flashes and bone loss (osteoporosis) are reduced by estrogen supplements.

The drop in estrogen occurs because the number of follicles decreases year by year as they degenerate with their oocytes. At birth, girls have several million oocytes in single-layered follicles. They are constantly lost until, at puberty, when cyclic ovulation begins, there are a few hundred thousand left. Each month about one thousand follicles degenerate for each one that is ovulated.

At the beginning of each cycle there are numerous follicles growing and secreting estrogen. Then as one follicle becomes dominant it makes almost all of the estrogen, as well as all of the progesterone, for the rest of the cycle. Since it only takes one follicle to produce most, if not all, of the hormones needed to complete the cycle in the ovary and uterus, there should not be any difference in performance between twenty-five-year-old and forty-year-old ovaries. It should not matter whether a woman has 40,000 follicles or 5,000 follicles if only one is needed to do the job each month.

However, laboratory studies suggest that as women's eggs and follicles degenerate over the years, each year's remaining follicles are less responsive to hormones than the ones that were lost or used earlier. In other words, the most unresponsive follicles are left unstimulated by normal amounts of pituitary hormones, and so are passed over year after year until they are the only ones left. When finally called on to perform, they are mediocre in growth and hormone production.

Because of the lower responsiveness of these follicles, ovulation is not as regular in the average forty-year-old as in the average twenty-five-year-old. Thus a woman in her late thirties is more at risk for primary infertility problems than a woman in her late twenties. The end of fertility often comes before menopause. Even if a thirty-eight-year-old follicle responds well enough for ovulation, it may still make lower-than-normal levels of hormones, resulting in luteal phase deficiency, LPD.

As I explained in chapter 10, LPD may be a natural occurrence in fertile women, and studies have shown that women have a poorly prepared secretory endometrium about 30 percent of the time. No studies have been done to determine the frequency of occasional LPD for different age groups, but women in their late thirties and early forties are considered at greater risk for chronic LPD than younger women. Thus they are probably at greater risk for occasional LPD.

Let us use some approximate risks of miscarriage for women who do not have any chronic conditions, to compare the chances for successful pregnancy in women over thirty five to women under thirty five. If we take the commonly considered chances of miscarrying due to chromosomal abnormalities, and put them together with an estimated chance of miscarrying due to an occasional case of LPD, then a woman under thirty five may expect to have six to eight months out of the year when conception will result in a successful pregnancy. A woman over thirty five may expect to have only four to five months out of the year when conception will result in a successful pregnancy.

These probabilities are worked out in table I. For both age groups, the chances of LPD are considered to be the same, 30 percent. But what if the chances of LPD are different between the two groups, as decreasing follicle responsiveness suggests? Then the number of months when the prospective mother over thirty five may expect a successful pregnancy after conception decreases from four or five to something less. It could be three or two or one. These calculations do not take into account differences in the frequency of ovulation that exist between women in the two age groups. Less frequent ovulation decreases the chances for conception itself.

Table I

The approximate chances for successful pregnancy after conception in women under 35 or over 35. First we calculate the chances of miscarriage due to chromosomal defects or LPD in a normally fertile woman. For this calculation I will use the following probabilities:

The chances of LPD are 30 percent. I use this figure because there have not been any studies relating the occasional occurrence of LPD to age. This translates to between 1/4 and 1/3, or three to four months per year. For simplicity I will consider one month equal to one cycle, so there are twelve cycles a year.

The chances of chromosomal defects range from 15 to 50 percent, depending on age. For women under 35 these are approximately 15-25 percent, which will be between 1/6 and 1/4, or two to three months per year. For women over 35 these are approximately 40-50 percent, which will be between 2/5 and 1/2, or five to six months of the year.

To calculate the chances of a successful pregnancy, we must determine the chances of a pregnancy that has NEITHER chromosomal defects NOR LPD. To do this,

---

we multiply the probabilities together:

Under 35:
- Chances of LPD are ¼ to ⅓; so the chances of NOT having LPD are ⅔ to ¾.
- Chances of chromosomal defect are ⅙ to ¼, so the chances of NOT having chromosomal defect are ¾ to ⅚.
- Chances of having NEITHER problem are (lowest) ⅔ x ¾ = ½ = 6 months to (highest) ¾ x ⅚ = $^{7.5}/_{12}$ = 7 to 8 months per year.

Over 35:
- Chances of LPD are ¼ to ⅓, so the chances of NOT having LPD are ⅔ to ¾.
- Chances of chromosomal defect are ⅖ to ½, so the chances of NOT having chromosomal defect are ½ to ⅗.
- Chances of having NEITHER problem are (lowest) ⅔ x ½ = ⅓ = 4 months to (highest) ¾ x ⅗ = $^{5.4}/_{12}$ = 5 months per year.

As women age, their fertility declines. Their reproductive systems have been exposed to the environment for a longer time. They have more time for damage to their uterine tubes to occur from infections. They have more opportunities for parts of their endocrine system or their ovaries to fail from autoimmune diseases, or for their ovaries to suffer from damage by environmental radiation, toxins, drugs, or alcohol. Even women who have led health-conscious lives since birth are subject to a decline in fertility from the loss of follicles and oocytes. Humans have a genetic program that cannot be tampered with in the short term. It is only subject to change over the longer time of evolution.

We can see this by looking at the changes in women's fertility compared to their life expectancy over the last 150 years. The average age of menarche, the beginning of menstruation at puberty, went from about 16½ in 1840 to 13 in 1960. This is attributed to improved nutrition and health of pregnant women and their young children. Healthy children grow faster and reach the size and maturity needed for sexual development earlier. For the past 30 years the average age of menarche in the United States has stayed at about 13, suggesting that this is close to the biological limit.

Over the same 150 years, life expectancy for women increased from 42 to 82 years, an even more dramatic change that also leveled off. At the same time, the average age at menopause has remained constant for all these 150 years at 50. There is probably a clock set in the oocytes during embryonic development. The fetus is programmed to make a certain number of oocytes. Then the oocytes are programmed to degenerate over time, without much influence of health and diet. Women who started menstruating at 16 in 1840 often died before menopause. Those who lived longer than average went through menopause at around 50. Women who start menstruating at 12, in 1991 and live to 85 will go through menopause at the same age as those women in 1840. This programmed loss of fertility is part of our genetic heritage, and every prospective mother over 35 is subject to the same decline in the numbers and responsiveness of her ovarian follicles, until she finally has only a few hundred left, and then these too are lost.

Here is an example of a woman who had her first child uneventfully at the age of 38. When her daughter was two years old, this woman and her husband started trying for their second child. Her periods had become very irregular, and it took almost a year to get pregnant. Then she had a miscarriage at about 9 weeks. This miscarriage was very upsetting. She experienced a feeling of being out of control that bordered on embarrassment, and deep sorrow over the loss of her planned baby. But this forty-year-old understood that her age was a factor. She knew other women her age who had miscarried. She and her husband continued to try to get pregnant, "trying like mad" to calculate all possible ovulation days in her unpredictable cycles. She got pregnant again about eight months later but had another miscarriage, this time very early, at 6 weeks.

The next month, while on a vacation out of the country, she had a painful ovarian cyst, and the doctor who examined her explained that it was a typical phenomenon in a woman beginning to go through menopause. She and her husband began to accept the fact that they would have one child, and that her fertile years had come to an end. The cyst worried her, especially a couple of months later when she felt very fatigued and her period did not arrive. Thinking this must be cancer or the final act of menopause, she waited a while longer, then finally went to her doctor. She laughed at his suggestion that he give her a pregnancy test in addition to other evaluations. Of course the test was positive, and she realized that she had not allowed herself to recognize all of her symptoms as the familiar ones of pregnancy. After waiting for the good results of amniocentesis, she and her husband finally told family and friends that a baby was on the way.

Not everyone is as lucky as this woman, and there are times when women have recurrent miscarriages before they are thirty-five. For some it becomes more and more difficult to get pregnant. The problem that caused the miscarriages develops, with age, into a problem causing primary infertility. Now worry over the possibility of miscarriage can cast a shadow over efforts to become pregnant.

If pregnancy does not come easily, a woman's doctor may begin some regimen to assist the process. Her obstetrician will try to determine whether she is ovulating and whether her uterine anatomy is normal. In these cases it is especially hard, but very important, to understand that miscarriage remains a real and normal possibility in addition to the problem of primary infertility. This is simply because women over thirty-five have greater chances of producing chromosomal abnormalities. LPD is also a possibility, and many fertility regimens include progesterone supplements, "just in case."

It is difficult to spend many years being in charge, and to plan for a family so carefully, only to be faced with miscarriage or infertility. As one woman explains,

We grow up with a belief in our inalienable right to parent. And in

our generation, we were going to have careers first, and when we
chose to have children it would not be a problem. Many women
who are facing infertility are choosing to do so later. And their
choices definitely have an impact on their fertility. So they feel a
great deal of responsibility. But nobody knew. Nobody told them.
They made the decisions based on ignorance, or inaccurate information. We can't hold ourselves responsible, but we do.

Suddenly an assertive, confident woman finds herself feeling needy, victimized, passive. She feels herself falling back on
her own mother's faith in the kindness and wisdom of doctors,
who will make everything better.

We come from an age where our mothers left it to their doctors to
tell them how they were, and I never really took personal responsibility for looking after my own medical state. I always thought it
was up to doctors to do it. And now I want to tell young women:
keep your own medical records, watch out for yourself. It's your
own body. Don't trust anybody else to keep track of it.

As another woman puts it:

I tend to be aggressive about most things, but I wasn't with my infertility, because it was so frightening. When there is no answer it
can be a nightmare. You feel when the news comes, you'll deal
with it. But when the news doesn't come, you have to make a
decision. One specialist suggested I might start thinking of alternatives to pregnancy. I didn't think I could face this, that it was
really possible that we were not going to be able to have children.
I had to decide, if I can't get pregnant, am I never going to have
kids? I might not be able to resolve my infertility successfully, but
I could choose whether or not to have a family.

People have to take control of their own infertility and their
own treatment. Because you are your only advocate, and the doctors aren't. Their agenda is different. They are into experimentation, they are into success, for all the right reasons. But it's not
your agenda. There are some things I resent about the way doctors handle things. But I haven't found it productive to be angry
with them. The bottom line is you have to love yourself, take care
of yourself, and understand everything you can about what
you're doing, and make decisions based on that.

Suddenly the shadow of age looms, where before a woman had seen an endless vista. It is a difficult time for a woman, and for her husband. All around her are friends and family with children, or babies, or swollen bellies. Across the table every night is the man who perhaps was not ready for a child a few years ago.

> My first husband did not want to have kids, but we had talked about having kids because he thought it might please his parents. Sometimes I think I should have tried to have children with him. All my life I've been waiting for men. I was married to him and he didn't want to have children. Then I married my present husband and he was in graduate school, so he wasn't ready to have children. I waited for him, and I was working. But I never really threw myself into my career because I knew that I would eventually get pregnant. So I never thought of my work as a "real" job. I never put my all into my work, and I know it affected my performance and success.

Many women in their late thirties and early forties have babies. What was considered a miracle "change of life" baby in the 1950s, giving teenagers a new sibling, is becoming more and more common as a first or second child. Many forty-year-old women have taken their fertility for granted, in fact going to great lengths over the years to keep from having a baby. Most women can have children after thirty-five, even after forty, without extra efforts. It may take longer to get pregnant than it would have ten or fifteen years earlier, but many women make up for their reduced fertility by having a better understanding of their cycles with more exact timing of ovulation.

It is important for women to know that their chances of miscarriage are high, and increasing every year, at a faster pace. If we look at any chart plotting the incidence of some particular chromosomal abnormality against the age of the mother, there is a slow, gradual increase through the twenties and early thirties. Then at thirty-five the rate of increase in occurrence of the abnormality starts to climb rather steeply. At forty it becomes almost vertical.

A woman over thirty-five who wants to have children must be aware that miscarriage is a very real probability, as is infertility. She is in a race against the predetermined demise of her reproductive abilities. The popular idea of a woman's biological clock is one of the most apt metaphors ever coined. The ticks and tocks are follicles dropping out, the best ones first, a thousand a month. It may take her longer to get pregnant than she expects, even with perfect timing of her cycles. If she is able to get pregnant, and determined to have a baby, the best approach is to keep trying and not let the tragedy of miscarriage put her off further.

Conclusion

A WOMAN HAS HAD A MISCARRIAGE. Her obstetrician has expressed sympathy, told her it was for the best; she lost a defective embryo. Her chances of success with her next pregnancy are very high. Right now she cannot think about her next pregnancy. The most important thing for her to do first is to let herself feel as badly as she needs to feel.

My advice to her is this: Do not let anyone tell you it was not really a baby. Do not let anyone tell you how to feel. If there are people who are embarrassed or uncomfortable with your grief, go away from them. Go where you can let yourself go. Let your tears roll. If your husband or friends or a support group want to help you ritualize your loss with a ceremony, do it if you want to. Your grief is legitimate. After you accept your grief, it is up to your individual nature what to do about another pregnancy. As a practical matter, time is always passing, but if it does not suit your needs, you should wait until you are ready. Learn what you need to learn. Plunging ahead is not always the answer.

Is there any more this woman can do? After a single miscarriage it will be hard to convince a fertility specialist to do a complete workup for her, even if she can find one who is not in such demand that an appointment can be made before she is pregnant again. But there is some self-examination that can give her clues about the possible cause of her miscarriage. Here are some suggested questions she can ask herself:

1) Counting from the day of her last period, how many weeks pregnant was she when she had the miscarriage: less than 12 weeks, 12 to 16 weeks, or more than 16 weeks? If the miscar-

riage was within the first 12 weeks, it is most likely due to a chromosomal abnormality, a one-time random accident. If it is before 10 weeks it could also be due to luteal phase deficiency (LPD), again, probably a one-time event. Between 12 to 16 weeks it is hard to pin down a likely cause. It may still be genetic, or it could be a multifactorial cause, including infection or anatomical problems in the uterus. After 16 weeks, incompetent cervix becomes a possibility.

2) Before the pregnancy, how regular were her cycles? If they only varied by a few days each month there is a good chance that her hormones were all at normal levels. This means she probably ovulated regularly and probably had a uterus that was prepared to sustain an embryo. If her cycles were irregular, varying by six days or more, then her hormones may not be in perfect balance, and she may have some deficiency or excess. This could mean she is prone to LPD, which would cause early miscarriages. It could mean she is not ovulating regularly because she is underproducing hormones, or her follicles are not responding well to hormones. It could mean her body is changing from a fertile to nonfertile, perimenopausal state. Has she experienced night sweats or trouble sleeping? These might signal thyroid deficiency or premature menopause.

3) How long did it take to get pregnant? The more regular the cycles, the easier it should have been. The longer it took to get pregnant, the more likely it is that something is awry. If her cycles were very regular but it took a long time to get pregnant, were there possible causes in her daily life, such as excessive stress, anxiety, sleep loss, ill health, or strenuous athletic training? These could all contribute to temporary hormone imbalances.

4) How old is she, and how old is her husband? If she is under thirty-five, there is less probability of recurring miscarriage. If she is over thirty-five, then her risk of making genetically defective embryos is growing every year. This is true to a lesser extent if her husband is older. But if she is over thirty-five, she is also at risk for hormone deficiencies, even perimenopause. At what age did her mother, aunt, or other women in her family begin menopause?

5) During the pregnancy, did she have an illness, fever, or unusually intense fatigue? This might signal an infection that could contribute to miscarriage. Was she exposed to any obviously harmful drugs or poisons during her pregnancy? Did she smoke heavily or drink alcohol regularly? Does she have diabetes, kidney disease, or heart disease? These may all contribute to miscarriage.

6) Did her own mother take DES while pregnant with her? Has any gynecologist ever discussed or tested her for unusual uterine anatomy, such as a very short cervix or shallow uterus, or septate uterus? Has a PAP smear ever shown abnormal cervical cells?

If several of the possibilities described above seem to apply, it might be a good idea to outline them in writing or thought and ask her obstetrician about them at the next checkup. A responsive obstetrician will then explain all the realistic possibilities she should consider. She can let her obstetrician know she understands that it is not routine to investigate a single miscarriage. But it may be that her individual story warrants closer inspection. She may have enough information to know she is a candidate for more miscarriages.

Obviously, this takes strength and determination, but the days of godlike doctors are over. Individuals must educate themselves and make reasonable demands of their physicians based on their individual needs. Doctors often treat everyone according to the average, but the squeaky wheel gets the grease, in medical care as in every other realm. And this woman cannot necessarily afford to wait.

Here is one way to help your obstetrician treat you as an individual: At the beginning of your next examination, briefly remind him or her of your history. Remind him how long you have been using a certain treatment and how long the two of you had planned to use it. Ask very specific questions. Get your obstetrician to think about your specific situation. Most obstetricians are very overworked and cannot spend all their time studying their patients' files. Each appointment suffers from a lack of time. Seeing many patients must become an efficient routine. Standard questions are expected and often answered patly. Ask questions that show you have information about your case that is helpful, questions that show you are an individual. Jog your obstetrician into thinking specifically about you.

It is important to remember that the only known cause of miscarriage is genetic and that this cause accounts for most single miscarriages. It is not certain that we will ever know whether the other conditions described in this book truly do or do not cause or contribute to miscarriage. Each woman may have a unique, multifactorial cause for her miscarriage. In practical terms, we really cannot know the answer.

The most common complaint women have about their medical care after miscarriage is that their doctors did not acknowledge their loss. Recently, women have been educating their doctors. Just in the last few years, obstetricians are realizing that, as one of them put it, "Miscarriage is not a small deal, and we shouldn't try to minimize this event." Some medical school instructors now teach their obstetrics students to take note of an individual's feelings and not make assumptions.

The similarity between women with infertility and women who miscarry is that they both have legitimate reasons for grief—the loss of children that are not to be born. But a woman who miscarries does have an advantage over an infertile woman. And that is that she can do something. She can get pregnant. Women with infertility, especially unexplained, are much more tied up with what their doctors can do for them with the latest technology. They have a difficult struggle with the realization that they must take charge at some point and decide whether to continue pursuing such treatments. For the vast majority of women who miscarry, there is no high-tech fix. But what seems like a disadvantage may really be an advantage, because it lets a woman see that she is mostly on her own.

After a miscarriage, it hurts when people say, "At least you know you can get pregnant." It hurts because it nullifies her grief. This statement denies her the right to mourn by suggesting that there was no loss. She must not let anyone nullify her grief. But after mourning her loss, a woman can realize that there is something she does not have to grieve. She is not infertile. She can get pregnant again.

A woman must ask herself some serious questions, and she must have confidence in herself. She must push for her goals, learn about her own reproductive potential. She must know her medical history, read, ask questions, think about any experiences that give her clues. Before shying away from another try at pregnancy, she might consider clues to possible infertility or continuing miscarriages.

A very small number of women who miscarry will go on to have other fertility problems. Their pursuit of answers and pregnancy must be done at their own tempo, according to their own needs and drives. Each woman must be honest with herself and understand her own expectations.

For a very small number of women, miscarriage is a wall that cannot be scaled or broken through. But for most women, miscarriage is a tragic but surmountable obstacle on a road that leads to childbirth. Most of us who miscarry can forge ahead with another pregnancy and be ready to offer our hand of sympathy to the next woman who miscarries on her way to becoming a mother.

Part IV

Appendices

Appendix A

Hormone Treatments of Infertility

AS WE LEARNED IN CHAPTER 7, the pituitary controls the ovaries and the ovaries control the uterus. The combined effects of hormones from the pituitary and the ovaries cause the egg to mature and be released, and the uterus to prepare for an embryo. In the absence of pregnancy, the ovaries and uterus are stimulated in a cyclic pattern. The pituitary gonadotropins, FSH and LH, rise to their highest levels just before ovulation, then fall to baseline levels and remain low until menstruation. The ovarian sex hormone estrogen peaks and falls once before ovulation, then again after ovulation. Progesterone begins its rise before ovulation, then peaks after ovulation. Estrogen and progesterone both fall to baseline levels just before menstruation. During the cycle the uterine endometrium thickens and develops secretory glands, then discards the extra layer in menstruation. Then the cycle begins again. In this appendix we will learn how obstetricians use an understanding of hormone regulation to develop hormone treatments for infertility.

Ever since the hormones involved in reproduction were discovered, physicians have attempted to find ways to use hormone supplements to control or enhance fertility. Birth control pills contain steroid chemicals with estrogen and progesterone-like qualities, though they are not natural hormones. Most of the substances used in contraceptive pills today are derived from a steroid found in a Mexican yam plant. Additions and modifications were made and tested for their effects. The first obstacle to deveopment of a birth control pill was that natural steroid hormones are destroyed by our digestive tract. Forms of hormonal agents needed to be manufactured that would be active when taken orally, so that women could take pills rather than injections. After that problem was solved, the right amount of estrogen and progesterone effects had to be generated. The object was to prevent ovulation without causing unmanageable side effects or irregularities in the behavior of the reproductive system. Most birth control pills in use today contain low doses of two agents: a progesterone-like component that suppresses LH secretion, and an estrogen-like component that suppresses FSH secretion.

Unlike the prevention of ovulation, induction of ovulation must be geared more to the individual, because different women can have problems in different parts of the hormone control chain. A woman with primary infertility or recurrent miscarriages due to hormone abnormalities could have a problem with hormone production in either the brain, pituitary, or ovary, or a problem with hormone response in either the brain, pituitary, ovary, or uterus. It is important for the physician to have some idea of which organs may not be functioning properly in an individual patient before prescribing treatment.

As an example, many women with primary infertility will undergo a post-coital test. This is simply a look at the quality of cervical mucus the woman makes around the time of expected ovulation. Normally the mucus made at this time is clear and elastic. In fact this is one of the few natural signs of ovulation that a woman may be able to observe herself. It is not proof of ovulation, but it signals the approximate time ovulation should be occurring The maximum flow of clear watery mucus follows maximal estrogen output, which occurs about two days before ovulation.

In addition to telling a woman or her obstetrician about the time of ovulation, the mucus can be studied more closely to see if it is good for promoting conception by being very stretchy, and by having healthy, mobile sperm in it when sampled several hours after intercourse. The mucus must be looked at in a microscope to observe the sperm. If the mucus does not stretch well, is not clear, or contains clumped or inert-looking sperm, it is not considered very good for promoting conception. A very small percent of infertile couples have a problem with cervical mucus as the sole cause of their infertility. This can be treated with estrogen supplements or circumvented by artificial insemination. Some women with poor cervical mucus still get pregnant, so high-quality mucus is not an absolute requirement for fertility.

The most common agent used to induce ovulation in women with primary infertility is clomiphene citrate, sold as Clomid or Serophene. Its main effect is to increase the secretion of LH and FSH by the pituitary. This enhances follicular growth, estrogen and progesterone production, and ovulation. Clomiphene is usually taken from days 5 to 9 of the cycle. Clomiphene is a nonsteroid estrogen imitator, with only some of estrogen's effects. The important feature of clomiphene is that it is taken up by cells and ties up the receptors required for a response to estrogen. Such receptors must be free for estrogen to have its effect. But clomiphene makes these receptors unavailable, so to the target cell estrogen is not there. Clomiphene occupies the receptors for weeks instead of the hours that estrogen usually occupies them.

Thus clomiphene fools the brain and pituitary into thinking that estrogen is absent. This leads to an increase in FSH and LH secretion, which ultimately results in ovulation. Clomiphene is also given for luteal phase deficiency (LPD), as I described in chapter 10. The object here is to increase stimulation of hormones during the follicular phase of the cycle, which adds up to a better luteal phase. In some studies clomiphene acts against estrogen's effects on the cervical mucus. Some obstetricians prescribe natural estrogen along with clomiphene to counter this effect.

One of the more notorious synthetic hormones is DES (diethylstilbesterol), another nonsteroid chemical that imitates some of estrogen's functions. Originally used to ease the discomforts of meonpause, DES was given to pregnant women who had miscarried previously or who threatened miscarriage. Although there was no experimental support for the use of DES to prevent miscarriage, it was thought to stimulate estrogen and progesterone production by the placenta.

In the 1950s, when DES was in wide use, there was almost complete ignorance of the mechanisms and complexities of hormone action. But the first babies born after DES treatment seemed healthy, and so the it-can't-hurt approach was applied. The tragic results of the widespread misuse of DES have been taken very seriously by many practicing obstetricians, who do not casually prescribe hormone supplements. The results of DES exposure were not known for many years, when the young adult daughters of DES-treated women began showing abnormalities. DES interferes with development of the fallopian (uterine) tubes, uterus, and vagina. The particular effect in an individual depends on the time during embryonic development that her mother took DES. A small percent of DES daughters have had life-threatening cases of vaginal cancer and have had major surgery to remove most of their reproductive tract, including the uterus. Many more DES daughters have a range of fertility problems, from minor to major, caused by abnormalities of their uterine anatomy.

Clomiphene is chemically related to DES, and in tests on mice it can cause abnormal development. However, it is given to women before pregnancy begins, and has been in use for over twenty-five years with no reports of ill effects.

The second-most-common agent used to stimulate ovulation is HMG, which stands for human menopausal gonadotropin. HMG is sold as Pergonal. It is a mixture of FSH and LH extracted from the urine of menopausal women who have high levels of these hormones because the pituitary is no longer controlled by ovarian hormones. HMG contains natural forms of the hormones and must be taken by injection. The effect of HMG is to directly stimulate growth of follicles in the ovaries.

Unlike the case with clomiphene, a woman may respond to HMG even though her brain or pituitary does not perform properly. But because of this circumvention of controls, women who are given HMG must be carefully monitored. Their ovaries can be overstimulated easily. HMG is commonly used to produce eggs for in vitro fertilization. A woman taking HMG usually has her estrogen levels monitored and ultrasound scans of her ovaries. In addition, a large dose of HCG (human chorionic gonadotropin) must often be given after several days of HMG, to act as a substitute for the normal LH surge that induces ovulation. Now I will explain the use of hormone supplements in the process of in vitro fertilization (IVF). A woman may be infertile because of a hormone deficiency or excess that affects her ability to ovulate, or because of conditions unrelated to ovulation. Her fallopian (uterine) tubes may be closed, so that sperm cannot get to the egg, or embryos cannot get to her uterus. Her husband may make too few sperm, so that the chances of any getting to the egg are small. The uterus itself may be an obstacle to fertilization. For example, mucus in the area around the cervix may be unfriendly to sperm, or the woman's immune defense system may destroy sperm in the cervix.

IVF is used to give women the opportunity to have biological children when they have damaged uterine tubes or unexplained infertility that does not involve ovulation. The best candidates for IVF are women who are under thirty-five, ovulate regularly, have regular menstrual cycles, and have been pregnant. Women who have not been pregnant are also accepted into IVF programs. There are still not many IVF programs in this country, and waiting lists are long. For this reason, women who seem to have too many obstacles to success are not accepted into such programs.

In IVF, eggs are aspirated (sucked out with a needle and syringe) or surgically removed from a woman's ovary when they are ready for ovulation. Sperm are purified from ejaculated semen. The eggs are fertilized by the sperm in a laboratory dish. *Vitro* is Latin for "glass," and refers to a process performed in a laboratory dish, outside the whole body. Embryos conceived by IVF still require a woman's uterus to develop to birth. The use of the sensational term "test-tube baby" is a misnomer.

Even when a woman is ovulating naturally, the IVF process begins with hormone treatments to hyperstimulate her ovaries. There are two reasons for this. First, normal ovulation produces just one egg, and IVF works best when several eggs are used. Second, timing of ovulation can be manipulated by hormone treatments, so harvesting of eggs can be made at exactly the right (and sometimes more convenient) time. Usually women are given clomiphene, three tablets a day, from days 5 to 9 of the cycle. In other regimens they are given HMG (Pergonal) injections over the same days.

The woman keeps a BBT (basal body temperature) chart, and the clinic monitors her estrogen levels beginning about day 8. The clinic also samples her cervical mucus and keeps track of her growing follicles by ultrasound beginning about day 7. LH levels are monitored every few hours when mucus and estrogen levels show ovulation is near. Eggs are harvested a day after the LH surge begins (about 26 hours). Alternatively, HCG can be given to stimulate ovulation before the body does it naturally with the LH surge. Eggs are harvested a little longer after HCG (about 32 hours). The eggs used to be harvested by laparoscopic surgery, a technique described in chapter 11. But more recently a less invasive technique has come into use. This is the use of ultrasound to guide a needle to the follicles and suck the eggs into a syringe.

After eggs are harvested, they are kept in culture in a laboratory dish for several hours. Sperm are separated from ejaculated semen, washed, and added to the eggs. After a day it can be seen if the embryos are dividing into two cells. Several embryos are introduced into the uterus after a few days in culture. The woman lies tilted for a few hours, and then takes it easy for two days. After another week she goes in for a blood sample to see if her HCG level is beginning to rise.

Here is the story of one woman who had successful pregnancies using in vitro fertilization after five years of infertility. After trying to get pregnant for several years, she began taking her temperature daily to see when she ovulated. Everything seemed normal, but tests showed that her uterine tubes were obstructed. She had laparoscopic surgery to open them up.

Her physician warned her that there was a high chance of having an ectopic pregnancy after such surgery, and indeed that is what happened. She had profuse bleeding and thought it was her period. But it did not stop, and she had to have surgery again to remove the ectopic pregnancy. The health risk of the ectopic pregnancy was very upsetting. This convinced her that she should try IVF. During surgery the doctor had seen that her other tube was badly scarred, and told her that her chances of having a child any other way were nil.

She was thirty-four years old, and saw an IVF expert on a talk show. She wrote to him, and within a few months she was interviewed and accepted as a good candidate for IVF. She had been pregnant many years before and seemed to be ovulating normally. For in vitro fertilization there are three stages. First, the hormone supplements are given to superstimulate the ovaries. Next, the eggs are harvested just as they are ready to be ovulated, and are fertilized in the laboratory. Finally, the young embryos are introduced into the uterus. She and her husband were told that there was some risk of an ectopic pregnancy. They were also told that the technique might fail, that the pregnancy might not "take."

Not "taking" means that although embryos are introduced into the uterus, for some reason the pregnancy does not proceed. This is a miscarriage. Since several embryos are introduced, it is a multiple miscarriage, one that happens to a woman who knows she is pregnant, earlier than most women know. But even anticipating this possiblity did not spare her from deep feelings of loss when her period started. "Every time it was a very emotional experience, like someone had died." She was supposed to keep still for two days after the embryos were introduced, but in fact was aware of every movement, and worried about it, for the whole two weeks after.

She has given birth to three healthy children in two pregnancies through IVF. For her first child it took three tries, which means that she miscarried early pregnancies twice and then went on with a normal pregnancy. The next time it took three cycles of hormone stimulation but only one embryo introduction. During the first two cycles her ovaries were overstimulated by the hormones, and the procedure was halted to avoid ovarian cysts. On the third try two of the embryos implanted, and she had twins.

In vitro fertilization does not always have such a happy outcome. Many women do not have children with IVF. Many cannot bear to go through more than one or two cycles of IVF. The wonders of technology can be very difficult for people to deal with in the face of such immense life crises. Here is the story of a woman who stopped after two rounds of IVF (the second was actually an attempt at GIFT, which stands for gamete-intra-fallopian-transfer, the introduction of eggs and sperm into the uterine tubes).

I knew all about IVF, and I felt very prepared. But nothing prepares you for IVF. It is often the end of the road, and it is a very intense procedure. There is so much associated with the need to succeed. And it is so disappointing when you don't.

When they retrieved the eggs, it was really magical. It was the closest I had been to success. They got ten eggs and eight of them fertilized. They put six embryos back in. It was incredible. Everything was going wonderfully. We called the six "the brood." We were attaching so heavily, and thinking we weren't; thinking we were handling it so well.

The period of waiting is just horrible. I had a sense that, "I've got to take care now. What I do is going to make this work." There is an overwhelming feeling that you have to make it happen. I went in for the early pregnancy test, then called from work for the results. Later I realized how foolish I had been. The test was negative, and here I was in the middle of work, devastated. I left.

I had planned I would try this three or four times. But while we were on vacation I realized I loved all children, and I could parent any child, and we should start looking into adoption. The second IVF was very hard, every minute, because every minute I knew it might not work. This time my husband called for the results, because I couldn't do it again. He called from work, sure he could handle it—came home twenty minutes later, devastated.

They went on to adopt a child, but something kept calling her back to fertility specialists. She finally realized what it was when she heard a woman speak about miscarriage or the loss of a newborn.

I knew that was my answer. I hadn't acknowledged that I had lost children. In the past I had said the IVF didn't "work." It was always a technical thing. I had never faced that those kids who were supposed to look like me and my husband were dead. When I could finally experience the grief I truly feel I knew I was finished with the fertility experts.

Because of the high-tech atmosphere surrounding IVF, many women focus on the success or failure of the procedure, only to learn later that they have forgotten to deal with the grief of miscarriage.

Appendix B

Glossary

amenorrhea
Cessation of menstruation for at least three expected periods.

aneuploid
Refers to a cell or individual with an extra or missing chromosome.

antibiotic
A family of chemicals that kill or inhibit growth of bacteria and mycoplasma. Sold by prescription in the U.S. Some are not considered safe to take during pregnancy.

antibody
A family of proteins that recognize and inactivate foreign substances that enter the body. Disease-causing agents and tissues from other humans are common targets of antibodies.

antigen
Any substance that can stimulate the production of antibodies when introduced into an individual.

blighted ovum
The remains of an embryo that died very early, leaving an empty gestation sac, detectable by ultrasound.

cervix
The long narrow "neck" of the uterus that connects it to the vagina and forms a barrier to infection.

chlamydia
A bacterium that infects the female reproductive tract. It is thought to contribute to infertility by damaging the fallopian (uterine) tubes.

chromosome
The physical site of genetic instructions in a cell. Each chromosome is a long chain containing thousands of genes.

clomiphene citrate
A nonsteroid chemical with some functions of estrogen, used to induce ovulation or treat luteal phase deficiency. Commercial names are Clomid and Serophene.

complete miscarriage
A miscarriage that requires no treatment, because the uterus is completely emptied, and the cervix has closed.

conception
The joining of sperm and egg; fertilization.

corpus luteum
The ovarian follicle after ovulation. It secretes estrogen and progesterone for about twelve days in a nonconceiving cycle, and for about three months in pregnancy.

D & C (dilation and curettage)
The most common technique for removing miscarried tissues from the uterus up to 12 weeks of pregnancy. The cervix is dilated and the uterus gently scraped.

D & E (dilation and evacuation)
A technique for removing tissues from miscarriages after 12 weeks of pregnancy. A suction device is used to clean out the uterus.

DES (diethylstilbesterol)
A nonsteroid chemical with some functions of estrogen. DES was

given to many pregnant women in the 1950s in attempts to prevent miscarriage. It causes defects in the developing reproductive system.

Down syndrome
A genetic disorder caused by the presence of an extra chromosome 21, or trisomy 21. Most Down syndrome embryos are miscarried and Down children are mentally retarded and have heart and respiratory problems.

embryo
The developing human for six weeks after fertilization, or until the eighth week of pregnancy.

endocrine gland
Any organ that secretes hormones to the bloodstream.

endometriosis
Presence of tissue that normally lines the uterus (endometrium) in a location outside of the uterus, such as on the ovaries or uterine tubes.

endometrium
The tissue that lines the uterus and engages in cyclic thickening in preparation for implantation of an embryo.

estrogen
A steroid hormone produced by the ovaries that stimulates the uterus to prepare for pregnancy, in addition to other functions.

etiology
The underlying cause of a condition.

fertilization
The joining of egg and sperm; conception.

fetus
The developing human beginning seven weeks after fertiliza-

tion, or about the ninth week of pregnancy.

follicle
A nest of ovarian cells surrounding an oocyte. The follicle secretes estrogen before ovulation, and becomes a corpus luteum after ovulation, secreting estrogen and progesterone during the menstrual cycle and early pregnancy.

follicular phase
The time between menstruation and ovulation in the ovary, when the follicle is growing.

FSH (follicle stimulating hormone)
A hormone made by the pituitary gland that stimulates growth of the follicle and assists in ovulation.

gene
An hereditary information unit, one of thousands on a chromosome.

gonadotropin
A class of hormones that stimulate the ovaries in women and the testes in men.

HCG (human chorionic gonadotropin)
The hormone detected in a pregnancy test. HCG is made by the outer layer of the early embryo and stimulates the corpus luteum to maintain the pregnant uterus.

HLA (human leukocyte antigen)
Substances found on the surfaces of human cells that cause an immune response if introduced into other humans, especially by organ or tissue transplants.

HMG (human menopausal gonadotropins)
A mixture of LH and FSH purified from the urine of menopausal women and used to induce ovulation. Commercial name is Pergonal.

hormone
A chemical messenger that travels from one organ in the body to another and signals the target organ to perform some function.

hyperprolactinemia
The production of excess amounts of the milk-stimulating hormone prolactin.

hypothalamus
A part of the brain that produces hormones that control the pituitary gland.

hypothyroidism
Production of less than normal amounts of thyroid hormone.

hysterosalpingogram
An X ray taken of the uterus and fallopian (uterine) tubes after they have taken up a dye. The technique can reveal the inner anatomy of the uterus and fallopian tubes.

idiopathic
Having an unknown cause.

immunization
A first-time exposure to an antigen by natural or artificial means. The body detects the antigen as "nonself" and produces antibodies and memory cells that provide for a faster response in the case of future exposure to the antigen.

implantation
The attachment of the embryo by its outer layer to the uterine endometrium beginning six to seven days after fertilization.

incompetent cervix
An abnormally short, weak cervix that is unable to remain tightly closed during pregnancy.

incomplete miscarriage
Expulsion from the uterus of some but not all of the products of
pregnancy. A D & C or D & E should be performed to empty the
uterus.

inevitable miscarriage
A miscarriage in progress. The cervix is dilated and the gestation
sac and placenta are moving through the uteus. It may become a
complete or incomplete miscarriage.

intrauterine adhesions
Also called Asherman's syndrome. Fibrous scar tissue on the
inner walls of the uterus.

IVF (in vitro fertilization)
The formation of human embryos in the laboratory for the purpose of introducing them into a woman's uterus for development.

leiomyoma
A benign growth in the uterus, also called fibroid tumor.

LH (luteinizing hormone)
A hormone made by the pituitary gland that stimulates ovulation and formation of the corpus luteum, among other functions.

luteal phase
The time between ovulation and menstruation in the ovary,
when the follicle becomes a corpus luteum.

LPD (luteal phase deficiency)
Usually refers to production of insufficient progesterone during
the luteal phase of the menstrual cycle resulting in a uterine endometrium that cannot maintain pregnancy.

meiosis
A series of two cell divisions occurring during the formation of
sperm and eggs. The result of meiosis is reduction of the usual
number of chromosomes in half so that when egg and sperm join

the embryo has a normal number of chromosomes.

menopause
The time when women's ovaries cease to function. There are no more eggs or follicles and hormone production has stopped.

miscarriage
Loss of pregnancy before the fetus can survive on its own, most commonly before six months.

missed miscarriage
The death of an embryo or fetus in the uterus without immediate expulsion from the uterus. Often detected by ultrasound.

monosomy
The presence of only one copy of a particular chromosome. Cells normally have two copies of each chromosome.

mutation
A change in a gene that is passed on to the next generation.

mycoplasma
A cellular organism that is simpler than a bacterium. Includes T-mycoplasma and ureaplasma that commonly infect the female reproductive tract.

nondisjunction
The failure of chromosome pairs or copies to be separated into different cells during meiosis.

occult miscarriage
A miscarriage that occurs so early that there is no delay in the menstrual period.

ovary
The organ in women that produces eggs and steroid sex hormones.

ovulation
The release of a mature egg from the ovary.

ovum
Scientific term for the mature egg.

oxytocin
A hormone normally made by the pituitary gland that stimulates labor contractions.

perimenopause
The time approaching menopause when pregnancy is still possible but fertility is reduced. Perimenopause is signaled by high levels of FSH.

pituitary
An endocrine gland that lies under the brain and produces many hormones, including FSH and LH.

placenta
An organ produced by a combination of the embryo's and mother's tissues that provides the mother's organ functions to the fetus, including nutrition and gas exchange.

progesterone
A steroid sex hormone produced by the ovary. Its main function during the menstrual cycle is to stimulate the uterine endometrium to specialize for implantation.

proliferative phase
The time between menstruation and ovulation in the uterus, when the endometrium is growing.

prostaglandin
A hormone produced in the uterus that stimulates uterine contractions.

secretory phase
The time between ovulation and menstruation in the uterus, when the endometrium is specialized for implantation.

septate uterus
An anatomical abnormality characterized by a dividing wall through the center of the uterus. May be partial or complete.

spontaneous abortion
The medical term for miscarriage.

steroid
A family of chemicals related to cholesterol, including the hormones estrogen and progesterone.

T-shaped uterus
An anatomical abnormality often found in daughters of women who took DES during pregnancy. The uterus is constricted and connections to the uterine tubes are narrow.

threatened miscarriage
Any incidence of light or moderate bleeding during pregnancy.

toxoplasma
A parasite found in uncooked meat and the feces of cats that causes severe birth defects.

translocation
Attachment of a piece of one chromosome onto a different chromosome. Normal individuals with translocations often produce defective eggs or sperm.

trisomy
The presence of three copies of a particular chromosome. Cells normally have two copies of each chromosome.

Turner's syndrome
The presence of one X chromosome rather than the normal two

in a female. Turner embryos are usually miscarried. Living Turner females are sterile.

ultrasound
A technique that uses sound waves to create images of internal organs, especially the developing fetus and the ovaries.

Appendix C

Sources of Information and Support

There are ever increasing numbers of local self-help groups for women and couples dealing with miscarriage, stillbirth, infant death, and infertility. Many women find talking to others who have gotten through the same experience very helpful. Personal networking is often the simplest approach to finding another woman with whom to share experiences. If this is not possible, a woman's obstetrician may be able to refer her to a group or individual. There are several national groups that have local affiliates. These provide educational materials and support groups. Some of the most widespread groups are listed below.

The Compassionate Friends, Inc.
P.O. Box 3696, Oak Brook, IL 60522-3696
(313)323-5010

DES Action
2845 24th Street, San Francisco, CA 94110
(415)826-5060

Pregnancy and Infant Loss Center
1415 East Wayzata Boulevard, Suite 22, Wayzata, MN 55391
(612)473-9372

RESOLVE, Inc.
5 Water Street, Arlington, MA 02174
(617)643-2424

Index

men's emotional
  response to, 9, 17,
  19, 20, 21, 51, 54, 55,
  62, 82, 85, 88
methods of coping with,
  60, 61, 62, 217, 218,
  220, 221
multifactorial causes, 220
multiple, 140, 145, 147,
  172
physical experience of,
  15, 16, 17, 18, 25, 26,
  29, 30, 31, 32, 33, 37,
  39, 40, 41, 42, 63, 64,
  79, 83, 86, 87, 205
physical process of, 38
physical reactions to, 9
recurrent, 11, 66, 70, 72,
  77, 78, 134, 146, 149,
  166, 167, 176, 177,
  187, 207, 213, 226
and women over
  thirty-five, 132, 166,
  169, 180, 205, 206,
  207, 208, 210, 211,
  212, 213, 214, 215,
  216, 218
and women's attitude
  toward medical
  care, 58
women's emotional
  response to, 9, 10,
  11, 15, 18, 19, 20, 21,
  45, 46, 47, 48, 49, 50,
  51, 52, 53, 54, 57, 58,
  59, 60, 61, 62, 65, 66,
  67, 68, 69, 75, 77, 80,

81, 82, 85, 87, 88,
  103, 105, 205, 206,
  217
Mourning, 20, 21, 22, 48, 52,
  53, 54, 61, 67, 68, 75, 76,
  104, 169

"Occult" miscarriage, 29,
  102, 107
Ovulation, 94, 96, 97, 98, 104,
  107, 108, 109, 110, 111,
  112, 113, 114, 115, 116,
  117, 173, 184, 210, 225,
  226, 227, 228

Physicians—and emotional
  support after
  miscarriage, 56, 57, 220
Physicians—and women
  who miscarried, 219,
  220
Physicians—treatment of
  women who
  miscarried, 21, 22
Pregnancy after miscarriage,
  58, 60, 76, 77, 78, 80, 81,
  82, 89
Pregnancy and women over
  thirty-five, 76

Recurrent miscarriages, 11,
  66, 70, 72, 77, 78, 134,
  146, 149, 166, 167, 176,
  177, 187, 207, 213, 226

Still birth, 53

About the Author

Kathleen Diamond has a Ph.D. in biochemistry with a specialty in molecular genetics. Her master's degree is in developmental biology. She has been a Fellow of the National Institutes of Health and the Molecular Biology Institute, and has lectured at UCLA on a variety of topics relating to cell and molecular biology.